27

Turandot

Giacomo Puccini

Opera Guide Series Editor: Nicholas John

Published in association with
English National Opera and The Royal Opera
and assisted by a generous donation
from The Baring Foundation

John Calder · London
Riverrun Press · New York

First published in Great Britain, 1984, by
John Calder (Publishers) Ltd.
London U.K.
and

Reprinted 1997 by John Calder Publishers

BRITISH LIBRARY CATALOGUING IN PUBLICATION DATA
Puccini, Giacomo
Turandot.—(Opera guide; 27)
1. Puccini, Giacomo. Turandot
2. Operas—Librettos
I. Title II. Adami, Giuseppe, III. Simoni, Renato IV. John, Nicholas, V. Series
782. 1'092'4 ML410.P89

LIBRARY OF CONGRESS CATALOGING IN PUBLICATION DATA

Puccini, Giacomo, 1858-1924
[Turandot. Libretto. English & Italian]
Turandot.

(Opera guide; v. 27)
Includes libretto in Italian by Giuseppe Adami and Renato Simoni, based on the play by Carlo Gozzi, with English translation.
'Published in association with English National Opera and The Royal Opera.'
Discography: p. 110
Bibliography: p. 112
Includes index.
1. Operas—Librettos. 2. Puccini, Giacomo, 1858-1924. Turandot. I Adami, Giuseppe, 1878-1946. II. Simoni, Renato, 1875-1952. III. Gozzi, Carlo, Conte, 1722-1806. Turandot. IV. Series. V. Title.
ML50.P695T72 1984 84-755966

ISBN 0-7145-4039-0

Typeset in Plantin by Margaret Spooner Typesetting, Dorchester, Dorset.

Printed in Canada by Webcom

Contents

List of Illustrations

The Genesis of the Opera

Mosco Carner

After the *Trittico* (*Il tabarro*, *Suor Angelica*, *Gianni Schicchi*) (1918) Puccini was, as usual with him after the completion of an opera, anxiously searching for a suitable new subject. There was the idea of a *Cristoforo Sly* to be drawn from the prologue to Shakespeare's *The Taming of the Shrew*, and indeed subsequently set to music by Wolf-Ferrari. Furthermore, during his stay in London in 1919, he saw, among other plays, Beerbohm Tree's dramatic adaptation of Dickens's *Oliver Twist* which seemed to him to contain strong operatic possibilities in Nancy's fate at the hands of Bill Sykes. This struck him so forcibly that he entrusted the fashioning of the libretto to Giuseppe Adami and Renato Simoni and they, in the spring of 1920, presented him with a fully versified first act and a detailed scenario for two remaining acts; it was to be called *Fanny*. But it was all wasted labour. Puccini rejected the subject, set as it was in London's underworld, out of fear that it might be too similar to that of *Il tabarro*.

What was the fundamental reason for rejecting these subjects? Puccini was in his early sixties when a noteworthy change took place in his operatic philosophy. A sentimental melodrama in a realistic setting, which had served him so well in previous operas, no longer corresponded to his new aspirations. As he informed his librettists, he now wanted 'tentar vie non battute' — 'to strike out on new paths'; his thoughts, he said, were turning in the direction of some fantastic fairy-tale, a tale, however, full of human emotions and moving the heart. It was in late 1919 or early 1920 that Simoni played a decisive role. Simoni was the editor of the prestigious literary periodical, *La lettura* (at one time edited by Puccini's late librettist Giuseppe Giacosa) and an authority on the Venetian playwright, Carlo Gozzi (1728-1806), about whom he had also written a play (1903). It was Simoni who suggested to Puccini to search for a fantastic subject among Gozzi's ten *fiabe drammatiche* or dramatic fables, and came up with the idea of Gozzi's *Turandot* (1762), a fairy-tale in five acts called *fiaba cinese tragicomica* (a tragi-comic Chinese fable), which by common consent was Gozzi's best and most human play. Puccini may have been conditioned for a Chinese setting by having also seen in London the musical comedy *Chu-Chin-Chow*, that great hit of the war years, and the melodrama, *Mr Wu* (later set by Eugen d'Albert). By March 1920 Puccini had read it and instructed Simoni:

> Reduce its number of acts to three, slim it down and make it effective, and above all heighten the passion of Turandot who has been buried for so long in the ashes of her great price.

Turandot had been set to music by at least a dozen different composers, the most famous being Ferrucio Busoni: he first wrote incidental music for an adaptation of the play by Karl Vollmöller for Max Reinhardt's 1911 Berlin production (from which Puccini was later to obtain some scenic material); and afterwards a two-act opera, *Turandot*, given together with his *Arlecchino*, both featuring the stock figures of the *commedia dell'arte*, in Zurich in 1917. There was also Giacosa's play *Il trionfo d'amore* (*The Triumph of Love*, 1875) which interpreted the Turandot legend in a much more modern psychological manner although the action takes place in a castle in medieval Italy; Simoni considered this play worth a close study. Puccini's first acquaintance with *Turandot* was not in its Italian original but in a re-translation of Schiller's adaptation for Goethe (Weimar Hoftheater, 1802) by Andrea Maffei, the same Maffei who made an adaptation of Schiller's *Die Räuber* (*The Robbers*) for Verdi's *I Masnadieri* (1847).

During the last four years of his life which Puccini devoted to *Turandot*, his working mood underwent, as never before, ups and downs fluctuating between elation and despairing self-doubt; elation because he felt that with this opera 'an original and perhaps unique work was in the making' compared with which all his previous works seemed to him a 'burletta' — a 'farce' — and that with it he was moving on to a higher artistic plane; self-doubt because of the novelty for him of a fairy-tale as a subject. Had he forgotten that he began his career with a fantastic, even supernatural tale, *Le Villi* (*The Ghost Maidens*, 1884), so that with *Turandot*, he was to come full circle?

Gozzi's 'Turandot' and its sources

Gozzi's dramatic fables owe their origin to a polemic against another Venetian playwright, Carlo Goldoni (1707-1793). Their bone of contention was the two-hundred-year-old *commedia dell'arte* — called the Comedy of Masks because the comic characters wore masks — adored by Gozzi and despised by Goldoni. Gozzi, the scion of a family of Venetian nobles, perceived in this ancient genre the most vital expression of the comic spirit of Italian drama and in particular regarded the Venetian *commedia* as the living link with the glory Venice had enjoyed in the past. But, by the middle of the 18th century, a new taste began to assert itself born of a more natural, more realistic mode of comedy in France. The spear-head of this movement in Italy (and its most successful exponent) was Goldoni, who, significantly, belonged to the middle-class. He saw in the old Comedy of Masks no more than a moribund art-form.

In the 1750s Gozzi began to arraign his rival in pamphlets and satirical poems, pointing to the triviality of Goldoni's plays, notably the introduction of types from the lower Venetian classes — gondoliers, washerwomen and fisherfolk. When Goldoni pointed to the crowds that were filling his theatre to see his 'realistic low comedies', Gozzi's retort was that 'any novelty, even Truffaldino and a dancing bear' would attract a large public. If Goldoni set out to depict human nature as found in real life — very well, he, Gozzi, would give the public something that was *not* natural — 'I shall stage a fairy-tale, one of those stories with which grandfathers and wet-nurses entertain the children on a winter's evening by the fire-side, and the Venetians will applaud me more than Goldoni.' His challenge took the form of dramatised fables: the first was *L'amore delle tre melarance*, *The Love of the Three Oranges* (1761) which established the model for all his later *fiabe*. The subject was an oriental tale decked out with spectacular stage effects such as speaking monsters, rocks, trees, and tempests with thunder and lightning. His protagonists were all of princely blood, involved in a series of fantastic adventures and love intrigues from which they always emerged triumphant.

The entirely novel feature of *Turandot* was the incongruous marriage of an oriental tale with the *commedia*. The idea may have been partly inspired by the experience of his 13th-century compatriot, the merchant-adventurer Marco Polo, who was supposed to have stayed a long time in China. Even more incongruously, the Masks spoke in broad Venetian dialect and their text was improvised from written-out cues. They were the mouthpiece of all

The three original Masks: Giacomo Rimini (Ping), Emilio Venturini (Pang), Giuseppe Nessi (Pong) (Istituto di Studi Pucciniani)

kinds of satirical allusions to people, customs and institutions in the Venice of his time — in *Turandot*, for example, to the inferior status of the Venetian women. The heroine's antagonism to the male sex springs, not from an atavistic impulse but from a rational and moral reason, namely the oriental attitude towards women as both slaves and the means for the satisfaction of men's sensual pleasure. Gozzi's Turandot argues her point in a long monologue before the whole Divan in which she expresses her conviction of her moral righteousness, although the method by which she tries to remedy this state of affairs — by chopping off her suitors' heads — is somewhat drastic. Having been transformed by Calaf's undaunted love to a woman of natural feelings, she comes to realise that it was her own sex who behaved with treachery and cruelty while the men evinced the highest degree of courage and generosity of heart — Calaf, by his offer to release her from her pledge of marriage, though he had solved her riddles; Timur and Calaf's tutor, Barak, by their readiness to sacrifice their lives to save the Prince's. The play closes with her admission that she had been sadly mistaken in her man-hatred and she says in her customary *licenza*:

Sappia, questo gentil popol di maschi ch'io gli amo tutti!	Know that, as for this kind race of men, I love them all!

Gozzi's play is dominated by two themes: the eternal war between the sexes and the transcending, cathartic power of true love, themes which are, of course, present in every subsequent treatment of the Turandot legend. And this brings us to enquire into the sources Gozzi may have used. He was certainly acquainted with *The Arabian Nights*, in which there are two stories bearing on his play — *Wisdom below the Severed Heads* and *The Splendid*

Tale of Prince Diamond — of which the first, concerning innumerable riddles posed to the Prince, is extremely dull.

Then there is a story in the famous *Il Milione* (1477), known in English as *The Travels of Marco Polo*. In it the Tartar princess Aigiaruc, a woman of gigantic stature, will only yield to the suitor who overcomes her in a battle of arms. The price the loser has to pay is a hundred horses; in this way she gains ten thousand horses before she is vanquished. Reading between the lines, we sense that, although the princess is in love with the last suitor before the battle starts, her pride will not allow her to yield. This seems to be the first intimation of the love-hate motive absent from Gozzi but clearly expressed by Puccini's Turandot. In the third act she sings:

C'era negli occhi tuoi	There was in your eyes
la luce degli eroi,	The light of heroes,
la superba certezza . . .	The proud certainty . . .
e per quella t'ho odiato	And I hated you for that
e per quella t'ho amato . . .	And for that I loved you . . .

This ambivalent motive exercised a strong attraction on Puccini (Anna in *Le Villi*, Tigrana in *Edgar*, Michele in *Il tabarro*); it culminates in *Turandot*.

That the Turandot legend was also known in Central Europe is also demonstrated by *Das Rätsel* (*The Riddle*) in the famous collection of German fairy-tales by the Brothers Grimm. Here the situation is reversed. It is the suitors who, obeying the Princess's decree, are compelled to pose the riddles to *her* and this omniscient maiden always solves them, thus sending the suitors to their deaths — until one day she encounters one whose riddle she is unable to solve, and they live happily ever after. Pointing to the same source in its close resemblance to the Turandot legend is the myth of the Amazons. One of its variants provided the basis for Heinrich von Kleist's verse-drama *Penthesilea* (it inspired Hugo Wolf to his tone-poem of the same name) which treats of the Queen Tanais whose country by the river Euxine is invaded by the Ethopian King Vexoris. His army plunders and burns the land, killing all the men and raping the women. The king forces Tanais to marry him but she stabs him to death on their wedding night, and this gives the signal for a holocaust of the invading army. As a consequence the Amazons establish a women's state with a new queen (Penthesilea) — who will only give her hand to the man who conquers her in battle — a parallel to Marco Polo's Aigiaruc. But the most striking resemblance between Penthesilea and Puccini's Turandot lies in that their man-hatred originates in the violence and rape suffered by an ancestress at the hands of a foreign invader. It seems most unlikely that Puccini knew this play, but it is possible that the highly erudite Simoni had read it. This motive — the rape and murder of Lo-u-ling — was introduced into the opera to provide a valid psychological motivation for the heroine's cruel decree. By the same token, the vow of Penthesilea to marry only the man who proves to be her superior in physical battle is matched by Turandot's vow to marry only the suitor who conquers her in a battle of wits.

A comparison of Gozzi's play with Puccini's opera shows a striking contrast in tone and feeling. Gozzi conceals the ferocious war of the sexes behind a charming fairy-tale of a naivety that borders on child-like innocence. In the opera, however, an atmosphere of sombre grandeur and barbaric cruelty prevails from the very beginning. For Puccini, the incarnation of this barbaric spirit was Turandot. Unlike Gozzi's heroine, she is presented as a goddess of destruction strongly coloured by Puccini's Mother-cum-Wife fixation (comparable to that of the Aunt in *Suor*

Katia Ricciarelli as Liù and John-Paul Bogart as Timur at the Vienna Staatsoper, 1983 (photo: Axel Zeininger)

Angelica). For just as Turandot drives Liù to suicide, so did the composer's insanely jealous wife Elvira drive their servant-girl Doria to poison herself in January 1909. I have little doubt that this real experience influenced him in his conception of Turandot and Liù. This image of Turandot is particularly striking in Act One where she is introduced as an apparition — 'come una visione' says the stage-direction — in fact as a hieratic, inaccessible, almost supernatural figure who sends the Prince of Persia to his death with a single imperious gesture. And it is a subtle psychological touch that Turandot preserves a sphinx-like silence in that act because it enhances her *singing* appearance in the second.

The unfinished opera and the character of Liù

There are several reasons why Puccini, despite four years of almost uninterrupted toil, was unable to complete *Turandot*. Compared with virtually all his previous heroines, Turandot was a most untypical character for him. With the exception of Tigrana and the Aunt in *Suor Angelica* (who may be described as evil), he had always portrayed sympathetic, lovable women; even Minnie in *La fanciulla del West*, if not exactly typical, belongs in this group. True, he had no difficulty in portraying Turandot as the cruel, man-hating tigress in her great Act Two aria. The stumbling block was the extended love duet of Act Three towards which the opera works as the ultimate dénouement. Puccini wrote to his librettists:

> It must be a great love duet. The two characters (Turandot and Calaf) who stand, as it were, outside the world, are to be transformed into human beings through love, and this love must take possession of everything on the stage.

Immense labour went into the verbal shaping of this duet and the text had to be recast four or five times before he was satisfied with it. Yet, significantly, the early part of the duet had already been conceived at least two years before the first symptoms of his fatal disease manifested themselves and gradually began to interfere with his work. This suggests that the cause of his inability to complete the opera lay deeper than meets the eye, and cannot be explained by the generally accepted view which is, namely, his premature death at the age of 66 — plausible enough but insufficient. There was, in my view, something in his psychological make-up that created an inner resistance to a total identification with a situation that proclaims the power of positive, all-conquering love. Puccini was, like Verdi, a born tragic composer but — in this quite unlike Verdi — a man with a pessimistic view of life. Of his twelve operas only one is a true comedy (*Gianni Schicchi*, 1918), in which he revived the spirit of the 18th-century *opera buffa*; *La fanciulla* only skirts tragedy with a happy end. But he was a composer naturally not given to a Happy End; even his lyrical comedy, *La rondine* (*The Swallow*, 1917), wrongly termed operetta, ends in sadness. His creative imagination demanded a stark tragedy, ending with a death or suicide casting its shadow over the whole work, in order to be kindled into full incandescence. And this brings us to the character of Liù.

Liù is essentially Puccini's own brainchild. Admittedly Gozzi provided a sort of model for her in Turandot's charming little attendants, Zemira and Schirina, and in Adelma, the Tartar princess who attempts suicide out of unrequited love for Calaf, just as Liù does with a fatal result in the opera. In the process of the opera's gestation Liù was transformed into a typical Puccini figure — gentle and frail, who yields wholly to love and dies for it. She represents a tragic element in the opera which is almost completely absent in Gozzi's tragi-comedy. Liù is born, in the last analysis, of the *Ur*-motif in Puccini's operatic imagination which he defined as the 'grande dolore in piccole anime' ('great sorrow in little souls'), a conception which clearly carries an overtone of sadism. She is the last in a line of Puccini heroines: Anna in *Le Villi*, Fidelia in *Edgar*, Mimì in *Bohème*, Cio-Cio-San in *Butterfly* and the Nun in *Suor Angelica*. According to my working-hypothesis, Liù's futile self-sacrifice is due to Puccini's unconscious equation of erotic love with guilt or sin for which the atonement must be death; this equation runs through all his tragic operas. Its true significance is to be found in the composer's neurotic compulsion to kill what he loved*. For Puccini, Eros and Thanatos were two sides of the same coin: they were the chief mainspring of his inspiration — the grit in his oyster.

It was Puccini who suddenly suggested to his librettists in the autumn of 1922 that 'Liù must sacrifice herself because of some sorrow, but I don't see how this can be developed unless we make her die under torture. And why not? Her death could be *a means of softening the heart of the Princess*' (my italics). Had her suicide (it takes place on the open stage and thus echoes the short-lived *verismo* of some twenty years before) actually been used to bring about Turandot's transformation, Puccini would not have been guilty of a serious flaw in the dramaturgy of his third act. We do not know why this important motive was lost in the final version. But we can put forward three explanations: (a) his neurotic compulsion to include a death scene at all costs; (b) that he wanted to bring about Turandot's transformation not by the death of a subsidiary character but by a sexual symbol — Calaf's kiss; (c)

* To explain this compulsion lies outside the scope of this essay; I refer the reader to pages 269-282 of my book on Puccini (second edition, London, 1974).

that leaving Turandot entirely unaffected by Liù's suicide would stress her inhumanity to such an extent that her subsequent 'humanisation' after the kiss would strike the spectator with redoubled force.

Liù's death and the following funeral cortège constitute, dramatically as well as musically, a scene of such finality that the opera might well have closed with it — an impossibility given Puccini's whole conception of the drama working towards the love duet. But the very fact that this thought suggests itself indicates the extent of Puccini's dramaturgical error: it makes the ensuing love scene appear superimposed. Puccini miscalculated by arousing our sympathies for the slave-girl and then, in almost the same breath, asking us to transfer these feelings to the Princess whom he had, up to now, done his Puccinian best to portray as a monster.

Rosa Raisa as Turandot, the role she created at La Scala in 1926 (Stuart-Liff Collection)

A possible solution might have been to let the curtain fall after the funeral procession has left the stage, insert a symphonic interlude describing the warring emotions in Turandot's heart and thus prepare us for what is to follow. (In the orchestral interlude between the two parts of the second act of *Butterfly* Puccini deftly achieved this kind of psychological transition by symphonic means.) It is arguable that this would have rendered us at once more sympathetic to and understanding of Turandot's capitulation as well as more responsive to her transformation. It is not beyond the bounds of possibility that, had the composer lived to complete the opera, and seen its first production, he might have revised it, as he did in the case of *Butterfly*. The love duet, in the much abbreviated second version of Alfano's completion which is normally now performed, comes perilously near an anti-climax.

Another factor that may have contributed to his difficulty with the duet was that, in the final act, Liù rises from a subsidiary role to be a heroine who directly confronts Turandot. In other words, at this juncture Puccini had to deal with two female characters diametrically opposed to one another in emotional stature. We encounter a similar situation in *Edgar* with Fidelia and Tigrana — their names are indicative of their characters — and in the less extreme contrast between Mimì and Musetta in *La Bohème*. This unresolved conflict is reflected in Puccini's own life by his wife Elvira and the servant-girl Doria Manfredi.

Some consider Calaf's reaction to Liù's death to be utterly callous in contrast to his father's lament. But Timur's life is wholly dependent on Liù whereas Calaf never loved her. It is she who loves him for the 'little smile' he gave her in days long past; in his aria 'Non piangere, Liù!' he only asks her to remain with Timur for the sake of that smile. In this light her suicide may be interpreted as the act of a girl whose mind has been greatly disturbed by her torture. From the moment Calaf sets eyes on Turandot he is, for his part, under a hypnotic trance which renders him oblivious to what is happening to others.

Alfano's completion

When Puccini died on November 24, 1924 he left behind a number of sketches for the last two scenes of *Turandot* — the love duet, and the final scene before the court and the assembled people of Peking. Toscanini, considered the sketch material extensive enough for the opera to be completed from it. Those responsible (Toscanini, the publisher Ricordi and Puccini's son Tonio) first thought to approach Vittadini or Tommasini, but the eventual choice fell on Alfano, a composer of the younger generation who had started his career in the Puccini-Giordano tradition and was later much influenced by Debussy.

What seems to have tipped the scales in Alfano's favour was the fact that Alfano (known in Italy also for two symphonies and some chamber-music) had great success with his opera, *La leggenda di Sakùntala* (1921) which deals with a Hindu legend; in other words, an exotic subject. Alfano delivered his completion of the Puccini opera in January 1926 — the première of *Turandot* was fixed for the last week in April — but Toscanini was dissatisfied with it because he felt that the completion contained too much Alfano and not enough Puccini. For Toscanini Puccini's sketches were, of course, sacrosanct and Alfano had not used every one of them. True, the relevance of some of them to the dramatic situation could not be established; and, although for the last scene Puccini had only indicated the

José Carreras as Calaf and Eva Marton as Turandot in Hal Prince's 1983 production at the Vienna Staatsoper (photo: Axel Zeininger)

brass fanfare, it was known that he wanted it to be based on Calaf's 'Nessun dorma' theme (Example 10). Alfano's task was quite considerable for he had to provide connecting links between the fragments, to compose new music for the transition from the first to the second scene, and to fill in the final scene. Toscanini forced Alfano, much against the latter's will, to reduce the first version of his completion (377 bars) down to 268 bars. At a contretemps between the two, Alfano is said to have made the ironic remark that if he was compelled to cut, he would resign from his post as director of the Turin Conservatory and take composition lessons from Toscanini. It is this shortened version that has usually been performed, and yet further cuts have even been made, notably the omission of the whole aria 'Del primo pianto'. I, among many students of Puccini's music, have always felt that Turandot's transformation is not very plausible from a psychological point of view because it is too abrupt, and that the final scene is not impressive enough to conclude Puccini's most spectacular opera.

Alfano's original was an organic and rounded piece in which Turandot's transformation took place *gradually*; it is therefore more credible than the revised version. A few examples will support my point. In the original there is, after Calaf's kiss, an orchestral explosion of 16 bars based on the 'Nessun m'avrà' theme (Example 9a) (but in the minor) from Turandot's second-act aria, to express the tumult in her mind at something that has never happened to her before. Again, after Calaf has revealed his name, there follows a *Presto con fuoco* of 30 bars in which Turandot reverts to her former self saying that now she knows his name, she has his life in her hands and will not bow her proud head to him. The stage-direction reads: 'Come se d'un tratto la sua anima fiera e orgogliosa si ridestasse ferocemente' ('As if suddenly her proud and haughty nature violently awakens again'). This unexpected reversal is far more in tune with her character than in Alfano's second version in which, after Turandot's words 'I know your name', Calaf at once breaks out with his tremendous phrase 'My glory is your embrace' (based on Example 13). From the original version of Turandot's third-act aria 'Del primo pianto' a total of 30 bars was taken out in several places. Alfano's beautiful offstage chorus 'Nella luce mattutina' in the transition music was also omitted. About the final scene Puccini had remarked that the 'revelation of love must come like a luminous star' (*bolide*) 'among the jubilation and acclamation of the people'. Alfano caught this image by making the exalted pair sing in unison 'amore!' and 'eternità!' on the high A, B and C against the full chorus intoning the 'Love' theme (Example 10).[2]

Certainly, Alfano's completion may be criticised in respect of harmony and orchestration, but any work left unfinished by its author and completed by other hands is liable to attract criticism, as witness Mozart's Requiem, Offenbach's *Tales of Hoffmann*, Borodin's *Prince Igor*, Busoni's *Doktor Faust* or Mahler's Tenth Symphony. Such a completion must always be in the nature of a second best. Yet these works have been accepted by a large majority of responsible musicians, to say nothing of the general public. No other than Puccini himself could have brought *Turandot* to a wholly satisfying conclusion, and Alfano's original ending is, in my view, a very acceptable *performing* version which enables the spectator to see and hear a conclusion that is dramatically as well as psychologically at any rate nearer to Puccini than the revised version. I cannot suppress a lingering suspicion that for Toscanini these aspects were of less importance than a strict adherence to Puccini's sketches, and that he took a hand himself in cutting down as much as possible of Alfano's own contribution. When a composer of talent and experience is entrusted with the task of completing another composer's work, he should be the principal arbiter of what to use and what to discard of existing sketches. We know that Alfano remained deeply embittered to the end of his life for having been forced to accept the mutilation, if not butchery, of what he had first delivered to Toscanini.

Toscanini and Mussolini

Turandot had its première at La Scala on April 25, 1926 when Toscanini laid down his baton after Liù's funeral procession, and turning to the audience said 'Here the maestro died' (or words to that effect) thus fulfilling the prophecy Puccini himself had made to him in despair in the summer of 1924. The performance closed at that point. It was at the second performance (April 27) that the opera was given with the abbreviated version of Alfano's completion. Because the first night might have nearly been wrecked by a political scandal of the first order, it is interesting to describe Toscanini's position at La Scala in the years from 1921 to 1929.

When the First World War — which Toscanini spent conducting troop concerts — was over, the Milanese felt that it was time to open La Scala again, since it had been closed in 1917. Tentative approaches were made to Toscanini to reopen the opera house under his direction, and he was prepared to accept on condition that it would not be leased to an impresario, as before the war, but run on strictly artistic lines. This led to the foundation of an organisation called the 'Ente autonomo' and the city of Milan then made over its ownership of the theatre to the 'Ente'. Though nominally acting as its artistic advisor, it was Toscanini who was in sole charge of its artistic policy. During his eight years at La Scala it was inevitable that

* This made a tremendous effect in the concert performance of the opera at the Barbican Centre, London in November 1982.

Francesco Dominici and Maria Zamboni, creators of the roles of Emperor and Liù in 1926 (Istituto di Studi Pucciniani)

sooner or later this musical autocrat would come into conflict with the fascist regime.

Toscanini seems to have met Mussolini first during 1917 when the latter was editor of the socialist paper, *Il Popolo d'Italia*. The paper was strongly anti-German in its views and castigated Toscanini for conducting works by Beethoven, Brahms, Schumann, Wagner and Strauss. Toscanini went to see Mussolini, had a terrible row and walked out of his office. Later, however, he (like many others including Puccini) saw in Mussolini the great patriot who, with various political reforms, would deliver Italy from its precarious economic situation in the aftermath of the war. Toscanini even ran on Mussolini's platform in the general election of 1919, when both were defeated. After the march on Rome in 1921, the foundation of the Fascist Party and the gradual suppression by Mussolini (now 'il Duce') of all civil liberties, Toscanini turned against him. Shortly after he came to power, Mussolini ordered that all public places were prominently to display pictures of the King and the Duce. While all other theatres complied, La Scala turned a deaf ear and Toscanini later proudly declared that under his regime no pictures of the King and Mussolini were seen there. In the autumn of 1923, a gang of young blackshirts forced an entry into La Scala where Toscanini was conducting Pizzetti's *Debora e Jaele* and ordered him to play the Fascist song, *Giovinezza* (a counterpart to the *Horst Wessel* song of the Nazis). Toscanini is said to have refused on the grounds that 'La Scala was no beer-garden' and 'no place for political propaganda'. By now he had become a red rag to Mussolini. The real clash came on the occasion of the première of *Turandot*, on April 25, 1926. Mussolini was to come specially to Milan to take part in the great fascist celebrations arranged there for Empire Day — April 21, the date of the birth of Rome. The management of La Scala considered it wise as well as their duty to invite him to honour the first night of *Turandot* with his presence. Mussolini, recalling the *Giovinezza* incident, would only accept on condition that the fascist song was played before the opera. But the political dictator did not reckon that he had to do with a musical dictator. Informed by the Scala management of this condition Toscanini confronted them with a curt ultimatum: either *Turandot* was performed without the *Giovinezza* or they would have to find another conductor. The management did not dare to replace the famous conductor, who was an immense box-office draw, nor postpone the first night of the opera to which critics from all over the world had been invited. Toscanini won the day — there was no *Giovinezza* to mar the baptism of Puccini's swan-song.

Giacomo Lauri-Volpi as Calaf and Maria Jeritza as Turandot, the first interpreters of the roles in America (Stuart-Liff Collection)

The Score

Mosco Carner

In Puccini's operatic thinking atmosphere and local colour played a very important part. They were, next to the operatic viability of a drama, his chief consideration in choosing a subject. Each of his operas is set in a different ambiance. Two things attracted him tc a very foreign subject. One was the challenge to experiment with harmony, rhythm and orchestral colour: it is no mere coincidence that in *Butterfly*, *La fanciulla del West* and *Turandot* he made his most noteworthy technical advances, or that *Turandot* is his most 'modern' opera. An exotic subject also afforded him the opportunity of using native tunes which were the fruits of his search for authenticity. (This characteristic of *verismo* seems to have begun with Giordano's *Mala vita* (1892) where original Neapolitan dance tunes were incorporated in the score.) With *Butterfly* and *Turandot* Puccini almost became a student of Far Eastern ethnography, consulting books on the customs and ceremonial of Japan and China and studying collections of oriental tunes. I have identified at least eight original Chinese tunes in *Turandot* (and seven Japanese ones in *Butterfly*) all based on the pentatonic scale which is the principal scale of Far Eastern music.

[1] Chinese Tunes

[a]

Ceremonial Melody

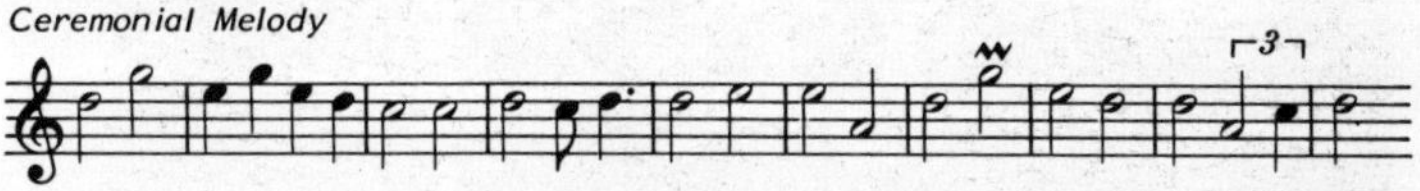

This is a ceremonial tune played on court occasions and also occurs in Chinese chamber music. It is first heard in Act Two, at the point at which the Emperor's standards are carried through the cloud of incense, in preparation for the Divan. It stands for the idea of legendary China, incarnated in the Emperor, and it is intoned in all the ceremonial scenes.

[b]

Moo-Lee-Wha

This tune entitled *Moo-Lee-Wha*, became first known in Europe at the end of the eighteenth century and is quoted in an English travel-book as well as in a German volume on musical history. In the opera it is chiefly used to denote the 'official' Turandot, the daughter of the Emperor. Its first appearance is in Act One, in the Boys' Chorus; it is, apart from the previous example, the most frequently used in the score.

[c]
Temple music : 'Guiding March'

This is a so-called 'Guiding March' characteristic of Chinese temple music and intoned at the entry of the Emperor into the Temple. In the opera it is associated with the idea of the Wedding and is first heard in Act Two, in the 'Pavilion' scene of the Masks.

[d]
Temple music

This again is a temple melody used in connection with sacrificial rites. It first occurs in the music of the Masks (Act One).

Ghena Dimitrova in the title role at La Scala, 1983 (Archive Fotografico Teatro alla Scala)

[e]
Hymn of Confucius

Puccini never uses this hymn in its entirety but only fragments of it on which he plays variations.

[f]
National Anthem

This is the modern Imperial Hymn, composed in 1912. In the opera the Masks make their first entry with it (Act One).

[g]
Folksong

[h]
Folksong

Both these tunes derive from Chinese folk-songs, which is possibly the reason why Puccini used them exclusively in the music for the Masks.*

*Ex. A is quoted from *Harvard Dictionary of Music*, by Willi Apel (Harvard, 1944). Ex. B is reproduced in *Travels in China*, by John Barrow (London, 1806) and *Geschichte der Musik*, by A.W. Ambros(Leipzig, 1883). Exx. C, E, G and H are quoted from *Chinese Music*, by J.A. Aalst (Shanghai, 1884. New ed. 1933); Ex. D from *Encyclopédie de la Musique*, by Alfred Lavignac (Paris, 1939), and Ex. F from article, '*National Anthems*', in *Grove's Dictionary* etc (op. cit.).

In addition, Puccini invented tunes in the *style* of Chinese music, a procedure similar to the so-called 'imaginary' folk-tunes of Bartók, Falla and Vaughan Williams. Such is Liù's moving plea to Calaf 'Signore, ascolta!' (Act One) in which the melody unfolds strictly on the pentatonic scale but bears the imprint of Puccini's own signature.

[2] LIÙ *Act One*

Occasionally Puccini added a semitone to the pentatonic tunes thus introducing a Western element, as he did in Liù's third act aria 'Tu che di gel sei cinta' which shows the features of a typically Puccinian *lamento*.

Puccini also uses the whole-tone scale which seems to have been first employed by the Russian nationalist composers, notably Glinka and Dargomizhsky, who associated it with the sinister, evil or supernatural. It made its entry into Western music through Debussy who used it, however, without these connotations. In Puccini it occurs for the first time, as though by accident, in the orchestral prelude to Act Four of *Manon Lescaut* (1893), but we encounter its frequent use for the first time in *Tosca* (1900) to symbolise the villain Scarpia. His characterising motif (anticipated in Act Four of *Bohème*) is sounded at the very opening of the opera, and Puccini does the same with the main 'Turandot' motif which is the motto of the opera and also built on the whole-tone scale.

[3] *Turandot*

Incidentally, the resemblance of Example 3 in melodic and rhythmic shape as well as in brass orchestration, to Iago's 'Credo' in Verdi's *Otello* is striking; it was, no doubt, the model. Example 3 undergoes a number of alterations in the course of the opera of a kind very rare in Puccini.

[3a]

Transformations of the *'Turandot'* theme

[3b]

[3c] *Act Three*

In endeavouring to characterise the Chinese atmosphere as closely as possible, Puccini went so far as to suggest an approximation to heterophony, a primitive kind of counterpoint in Eastern music where the same melody is repeated by several instruments in variations.

[4] *Act Three*

The trumpets have the pentatonic tune while the woodwind play the same five notes in the harmony and the violins and harp unfold them horizontally.

The harmonic language of *Turandot* is the most advanced of Puccini's works. He kept well abreast of the technical innovations of his time (notably those of Stravinsky and Richard Strauss) and we find bitonality, for example, in the Mandarin's reading of Turandot's decree: the D minor chord is sounded together with the C# major chord, and subsequently the B*b* major chord with that of A major, and the resulting fierce dissonances underline the cruelty of the proclamation. A particularly striking example of bitonality is to be found at the opening of the Masks' solo scene in Act Two which is based on the two modes, a semitone apart, of the whole tone scale, evidently intended to denote their grotesque aspect.

[5] *The Three Masks, Act Two*

As will be seen from the above example, integral to the whole-tone scale is the augmented fourth or tritonus, called the *diabolus in musica* by medieval theorists because of the difficulty for singers to pitch this dissonant interval correctly; after *Butterfly* (1904) it occurs with increasing frequency in

Puccini's operas. By the same token the particular atmosphere of *Turandot* invites an extremely high level of dissonant configurations, as in the shouts of the crowd for Pu-Tin-Pao and the voices of the dead suitors.

[6] CHORUS

The Dead Suitors

Equally characteristic of Puccini's last opera are polyrhythmic passages:

[7] *Act One*

Here each of the seven instruments employed (oboe, drums, tambourine, tam-tam, celesta, solo violin and violoncello) plays a different rhythm and Stravinsky's influence can be felt. (Example 7 represents a reduced version of the passage in the full score.) Puccini's orchestration is a study in itself for the score is a most fascinating essay in instrumental exoticism. The orchestra is the largest he ever employed and, as in authentic Chinese music, the percussion is very prominent. There are about a dozen different percussion instruments in the main orchestra (timpani, triangle, tambourine, bass drum, cymbals, tam-tam, Chinese gong, glockenspiel, bells, celesta and two xylophones — one of them is a bass xylophone which had to be especially built); added to this is the stage band for the court scenes (2 saxophones, 6 trumpets, 4 trombones, tambourine and tam-tam). With the possible exception of *La fanciulla del West*, in no other of Puccini's operas does the orchestra play such an important part in evoking an atmosphere and underlining key points in the drama. Nonetheless, the composer remains faithful to the tradition of Italian opera by leaving the hegemony in this intricate texture to the singers. Broadly speaking, certain instrumental groups tend to be associated with certain characters — the heavy brass with the court scenes (the Emperor and his retinue), wind and strings with Turandot, the warm strings mostly with Calaf, while for Liù, the lyrical role *par excellence*, Puccini reserves the most delicate tints of his orchestral palette: exquisite brush-strokes of solo flute, oboe and violin. The Masks disport themselves to the dry crackle of upper woodwind, punctuated by pizzicato string harmonics, glassy celesta chords and rattling xylophone passages and, at times, the squeaks of piccolo and muted trumpets.

Turandot is a choral opera in which the massed voices play an important and, as in Act One, an active part in the drama. Similar to the chorus of the gold-miners in *La fanciulla*, the crowd generates a savage atmosphere, notably in Act One where its orchestral theme stands also for the Executioner:

[8]

Melody, key and rhythm at once recall Mussorgsky's song *Gopak*, as indeed the treatment of the chorus in general calls to mind *Boris Godunov*, which Puccini is likely to have heard at La Scala in 1909.

The characterisation of the protagonists

Of Turandot's leitmotif (Example 3) we have already spoken in connection with Puccini's use of the whole-tone scale. To this must be added the pentatonic tune entitled *Moo-Lee-Wha* (Example 1b). A full portrayal of the Princess is drawn in her aria 'In questa Reggia'. The length of this aria (70 bars) and its technical difficulty are in themselves a means to characterise her as a goddess of destruction. It consists of two sections reminiscent of the Recitative and Aria in 18th-century opera. The first section is devoted to the story of the ancestress which explains Turandot's vow. Written in a declamatory ballad-like style there is a visionary quality to the vocal line that is enhanced by hushed choral interjections. When Turandot arrives at the point at which she refers to the many princes on whom she has avenged the death of Lo-u-ling, her agitation culminates in — 'that cry, that death!'. Cast in one of Puccini's favourite keys, G*b*, it is one of the great tunes of the opera, one of magnificent sweep and range.

[9a]

[9b] TURANDOT *Act Two*

After repeating her vow not to yield herself to a man, she rises to menacing grandeur the pregnant phrase 'Gli enigmi sono tre, la morte è una!' ('The riddles are three, death is one!'). The theme is little more than a bar long (Example 9b) and is treated in rising sequences — E*b* major-F# major

(Calaf) — A*b* major. (In a sketch dating from as late as February 1924 Puccini tried to develop this idea into a period of 2×8 bars in, respectively, F major and A major, which conveys the tension far less impressively than the shorter final version.) With Calaf's entry and his subsequent unison with Turandot the orchestra doubles the vocal line: it is one of the most powerful effects in his whole *oeuvre*. 'In questa Reggia' is a gruelling test for the soprano on account of its leaps down a ninth, and of its high tessitura (top A, A*b*, B and C), the vocal line lying for the most part around the awkward voice-break between the middle and the high soprano register (E-F). Here (as elsewhere) one senses the influence of the Strauss of *Salome* (1905), *Elektra* (1909) and *Die Frau ohne Schatten* (1919).

Turandot's second aria 'Del primo pianto', sung in the love duet with Calaf (Act Three) is psychologically important because it gives the first sign of her transformation. Regrettably, this aria has frequently been cut in performance.

Unlike Turandot, Calaf has no pervasive leitmotif. It is not until the point when he poses *his* riddle to the Princess that he becomes associated with a melody of his own — the 'Name' or 'Love' theme; Puccini's use of it suggests that these two terms were interchangeable in his mind.

[10] *The 'Name' or 'Love' theme*

This assumption is supported by the fact that this ardent theme forms the basis of his third-act *romanza* 'Nessun dorma' ('None shall sleep') and is introduced by Alfano, as Puccini intended, in the final scene to symbolise the apotheosis of love. Calaf is, like Turandot, conceived in the heroic mould but his music is at once warmer, more expressive and suppler of vocal line. It displays a virile fibre absent from Puccini's other tenor heroes, with the exception of Johnson in *La fanciulla* and Luigi in *Il tabarro*. The hysterical outbursts of Cavaradossi are entirely absent.

In Act One Calaf is an impetuous young prince possessed by his resolve to undergo the test of Turandot's riddles. Yet his tender feelings are expressed in his aria 'Non piangere, Liù', ('Don't cry, Liù'), another *lamento* typical of Puccini, with certain similarities to Liù's third-act aria (Example 12): the same key (E*b* minor), the same dirge-like opening with monotonously repeated chords and the tendency of the vocal line to droop. One or two turns recall Butterfly's farewell to her child. The two situations are akin, for 'Non piangere, Liù' is, in a sense, a farewell to Liù, a child, one imagines, of no more than 15 years. In an entirely different vein is 'Nessun dorma', when Calaf dreams of victory over Turandot. Softly he takes up the heralds' cries that sound through the night, Puccini evoking the nocturnal atmosphere with delicate orchestral timbres. As his ardour grows, he intones the 'Love' theme (Example 10) doubled by the cellos in the lower octave which lends the tune a lovely mellowness; the repetition of the long-arched melody by the off-stage women's chorus is a signally poetic touch. 'Nessun dorma' has a noble lyrical beauty that singles it out from Puccini's other tenor arias.

As for Liù, she is the only character in the opera to move our hearts — a

Mimi or Butterfly transferred from realistic surroundings to a legendary China. Her part bears the stamp of deeply-felt inspiration. It may seem strange that she does not have a theme of her own — possibly because she is, after all, a subsidiary figure. There is, however, a theme which, to judge from the contexts in which it occurs, is associated with her and Timur.

[11]

This plangent melody is first heard in Act One, in the scene where the guards push back the crowd, and when many get trampled in the ensuing panic. Example 11 does not on the surface fit the brutal scene and only makes sense if we relate it to Liù's anxiety for Timur, whose sole companion

Mafalda Favero as Liù and Corrado Zambelli as Timur at Covent Garden in 1939 (BBC Hulton Picture Library)

Maria Pellegrini as Liù at Covent Garden in 1967 (photo: Reg Wilson)

Lotte Schöne as Liù, the first to sing the role at Covent Garden, in 1927 (Royal Opera House Archives)

she is. This interpretation finds support in the fact that the second and last occurrence of Example 11 is in Act Three in which Liù and Timur are dragged before Turandot in order to make them reveal the name of the Unknown Prince. Example 11 has a strong family likeness to the melody accompanying Scarpia's writing of Tosca's safe-conduct and his subsequent murder (*Tosca*, Act Two): note the similarity of the melodic and rhythmic patterns, the same scoring (strings in octave) and the same key (F# minor). For stylistic reasons I am much inclined to date both these melodies to a much earlier period, possibly to the time of *Manon Lescaut*.

Liù has three arias, the first of which occurs in Act One and the last two in Act Three. 'Signore, ascolta!' ('Lord, listen!', Example 2) and 'Tanto amore segreto' ('Such love — secret and unconfessed', Act Three) are, appropriately for this diminutive character, cavatinas rather than full-blown arias. Her first aria is strictly pentatonic, the vocal line being formed of tiny five-tone motifs ranged in a kaleidoscopic fashion and supported by solo woodwind and muted violins. The effect recalls the limpid delicacy of a Chinese pen-drawing. It introduces Liù as a gentle and warm-hearted creature whose despairing passion for Calaf finds poignant expression in her phrase 'Liù non regge più! Ah, pietà!' ('Liù can stand no more! Ah, pity!') which is marked by two leaps upwards to top A and B, respectively. Of more or less the same cast is her third-act 'Tanto amore segreto' in which she openly declares her love for the Prince. It is, however, in her farewell aria 'Tu che di gel sei cinta' ('You who are girded with frost') that the composer wrote his most poignant music for her. As with Cavaradossi's 'E lucevan le stelle' (*Tosca*, Act Three), the music for it leapt into his mind before he was in possession of the final version of the text. When two years later he requested Adami to provide him with two seven-syllable verses, it was his own dummy verses (Puccini's expression for it was '*forma maccheronica*'), though not always in a seven-syllable metre, that were adapted to the music as they stood. The aria displays all the characteristics of a *lamento*; the vocal line is enhanced by its exotic orchestration. The *crescendo* of emotions reaches its climax in the heart-rending phrase 'per non vederlo più' ('never to see him again') and is mirrored in Puccini's scoring in a rising terrace of sound (oboe-bassoon; oboe - cor anglais - strings; full orchestra). Nor should we overlook the subtlety of the phrasing: the true phrasing would be in a regular 6/4 metre, but by harnessing the vocal melody to an alternating 2/4 and 4/4, the sense of an irregular metre obviates the deadening effect of a regular accentuation.

[12] LIÙ *Act Three*

(The thought cannot be suppressed that Puccini modelled this melody on the 'Augures printaniers' in Stravinsky's *Sacre du printemps*.) It was an inspiration to continue Liù's music into the scene of mourning for her, when Calaf and Timur join their voices to the superstitious crowd praying for forgiveness from her shade; even the Masks are moved. The scene closes with a procession carrying the little body into the night and the chorus fading into silence, the result is one of the most poignant in all opera.

There remain the three Masks. Puccini treats them as a kind of miniature chorus singing the same music, like the relatives in *Gianni Schicchi*. They may be differentiated by their voices, Ping being a baritone and Pang and Pong tenors of a light calibre somewhat recalling the *tenore di grazia* of the old Italian *opera buffa*. They often fall into a conversational tone which sharply distinguishes them from the other characters. They have no leitmotifs; instead they are characterised by short pentatonic figures mostly derived from Examples 1d, f, g and h. Characteristic too is the prevailing *ballabile* style of their music, for example the dance-like *scherzo* 'Fermo! Che fai?' ('Stop! What are you doing?') with which they fling themselves across Calaf's path in order to prevent him striking the gong (Act One). In addition, the skipping intervals in the vocal parts, jerky rhythms and *sec*, brittle orchestration create the image of puppets at once comically grotesque and malevolent. Puccini evidently became so strongly attracted to the Masks that, in spite of first wanting to eliminate them altogether, he gave them a scene all of their own in Act Two. This might at first seem superfluous because it retards the action, like a ballet *divertissement* inserted for the audience's delectation. Yet in the context of this opera it does serve two essential purposes — one psychological, the other dramatic. Something like human emotions surges up in the dessicated hearts of the three courtiers and, on the other hand, it provides a most welcome relief from the sombre drama. It appears to be an effortless and enchanting piece of *chinoiserie*, for all that the composer laboured over it. We almost hear him chuckle in it — a half ironic, half delighted chuckle. The effect of the whimsical humour springs partly from his deft manipulation of snatches of authentic and self-invented Chinese tunes, partly from the orchestration and partly from the changes in vocal delivery. Thus the Masks are made to sing now mysterious and serious, now gay and with 'comic desolation', now *staccato*, now *legato*, now with *falsetto*, now with closed mouths, now loud, now *dolce* in *mezza voce*. Puccini, by his detailed markings, leaves nothing to chance in order to achieve his intended effect of drollery and grotesqueness. Exotic *jeu d'esprit* has rarely been played with nimbler and more loving hands.

The 'Riddle' scene

The scene of the Masks is followed by the 'Riddle' scene which is the first of the opera's two *peripeteiae* (the second is the love duet of Act Three). For the decisive contest between Turandot and Calaf Puccini plays out his trump card with careful deliberation and an admirable sense of timing. There is, first, the aged Emperor's vain attempt, in a blanched voice, to dissuade the Prince from his resolve, his speech being almost entirely unaccompanied, with just a few punctuations by the orchestra. This is followed by the Mandarin's proclamation of Turandot's decree and the scene is set for her monologue 'In questa Reggia': all this as an exordium to the riddles.

Commentators have criticised the fact that Turandot's three riddles and Calaf's answers are set to the same music and one of them (Richard Specht) wondered why Puccini, with his inborn sense of the theatre, did not give pictorial expression to each one so as to heighten suspense and make a musical *crescendo*, instead of the 'stately monotony which ends by exasperating our nerves'. Puccini must have considered some such solution. Why then did he eschew it? Specht saw in this a 'fourth riddle' added to Turandot's three. But there seems to me a valid answer to it. Turandot poses the riddles in a ritual, which she has performed with each of her suitors — according to Gozzi, there have been ninety-nine before Calaf. It is characteristic of ritual that its hieratic rigidity and sameness creates an effect hypnotic in its monotony, and it is precisely this which Puccini sought to achieve. Moreover, he seems to have taken for model the 'Judgement' scene in Act Four of *Aida* where the Priest addresses Radamès three times to the same music; the only difference is that Verdi raises each repeat a semitone higher while Puccini does this only in Turandot's third riddle. Another parallel with Verdi lies in the way Puccini separates the three riddles by the Eight Wise Men confirming each of the correct solutions, just as Amneris prays for Radamès's salvation after each of the Priest's three charges and the trumpet calls at the opening of each scene.

But it must be admitted that although the music for this scene is functional rather than inspired, it fits the dramatic situation like a glove. The formula for the riddles, derived from the 'Turandot' motif is:

[13]

(Alfano in his completion of Act Three uses this motif for Calaf's 'La mia gloria è il tuo amplesso', 'My glory is your embrace'.) Both Turandot and Calaf's parts are declamatory and only sparsely underlined in the orchestra so that the crucial words may be distinctly heard. Yet there are a number of subtle instrumental touches to add point to the words: the muted horns and trumpets for the stabbing Example 13, the *appoggiature* at 'come un lamento' ('like a painful sigh'), the nervous flicker of string arpeggios at Turandot's 'Gelo che ti dà fuoco!' ('Frost that sets you afire!'), the cold, glassy sound of the combined glockenspiel, celesta and harp at her 'del tramonto il vivido baglior!' ('the vivid glow of the sunset!'). Noteworthy too are such symbolic details as when Turandot descends a step down the majestic staircase after each of Calaf's solutions of her riddles (not in Gozzi). Calaf also begins his riddle with Example 13, but then the orchestra turns to the noble melody of the 'Love' theme, Example 10. With the background of splendour and pomp against which the two protagonists measure their strength against each other — the Emperor seated high on the throne at the top of the staircase like an idol, the courtiers in their multi-coloured ceremonial costumes, the agitated populace waving flags and banners — the 'Riddle' scene is eloquent testimony to Puccini's eye for stage spectacle.

The Musico-Dramatic Structure of Act One

The first act of *Turandot* must, in respect of musico-dramatic structure, be considered the best of all Puccini's opening acts. Its striking feature is a large-scale design the composer had never attempted before, a design broadly resembling that of a symphony in four movements, and held together by a central mood. Using symphonic terminology we may describe the opening scene, the Mandarin's reading of Turandot's decree, as the 'slow introduction'; the *Allegro* is a mainly choral movement extending to the close of the chorus 'Ungi, arrota!'; its general character is one of ferocity, its basic tempo fast and its main key F# minor. The following *Andante* opens with the choral apostrophe to the moon, impressionist in colour, and closes with the funeral march of the Persian Prince. The music is partly evocative (as in the 'Moon' chorus), partly dramatic in a sombre vein, generally slow, and its chief tonalities are D major and E*b* flat minor, the latter characteristic of the opera as a whole. So far the music has been dominated by the chorus; from now on the soloists take the lead. A brief transition — the exchanges between Calaf and Timur — leads to the *scherzo* of the Masks: light and capricious of mood, its basic rhythm is 3/4 and major keys predominate. The first part of this *scherzo* is an almost self-contained piece in ternary form firmly anchored in A*b* major. Even two contrasting Trios may be discerned: the first is the chorus of Turandot's maids bidding the Masks to be silent (an *Andante lento* in C# minor and poly-rhythmic, [7] and the second is the eerie chorus of the dead suitors [6] (a *Lento* resting on a bass pedal A-F#). After the *scherzo*, another transition — Timur's appeal to his son to desist from his reckless venture — leads to the

'Turandot' at Covent Garden: Walter Midgley as Calaf (1947), Joseph Ward as the Emperor (1963) (photo: Houston Rogers)

Finale, which is the crowing movement of Puccini's 'symphony'. It comprises Liù's aria 'Signore, ascolta!' and that of Calaf's 'Non piangere, Liù', the last two bars of which contain the cell from which the ensuing Finale is organically developed. The emotional curve of this great ensemble in E♭ minor rises from the plangent lyricism of the two arias to a powerful tension (*p*, *ma con calore crescente*) in a measured tempo.

Such large-scale design — four distinct sections, each with its own material, its own rhythm and tonalities, yet the whole anchored in a central mood — can hardly be regarded as coincidence. Indeed, it argues a deliberate plan testifying to the composer's consummate power of dramatic organisation in his last period. The final chorus is easily Puccini's most impressive essay in the handling of concerted voices and was anticipated as early as 1893 in the 'Embarkation' finale of Act Three of *Manon Lescaut*, also in the key of E♭ minor. Like that early ensemble, that of *Turandot* springs directly from the action — Liù, Timur, the Masks and chorus join in a last desperate effort to prevent the Prince striking the gong. (The detail of this scene was sketched out by Puccini as early as December 1921 and with a few minor alterations retained in the final version.) Dramatic suspense is built up by a masterly treatment of the voices. The six soloists toss fragments of the rolling, heaving theme from one to the other until at the psychological moment an invisible chorus and a brass orchestra enter to heighten the tension until the climax of Calaf's thrice-repeated cry 'Turandot!' dramatically answered by the choral 'La morte!'. Nothing less than overwhelming is the following section when, after Calaf's three gong strokes, the stately 'Turandot' theme (Example 1b) is intoned in the glorious radiance of D major; after so much E flat minor the sudden shift down a semitone to the major key creates a stupendous dramatic effect. Even the Verdi of *Otello* did not pen a greater finale. Acts Two and Three, looser in structure, resemble a more suite-like design.

The 'Riddle' scene in Chini's design for the first production at La Scala in 1926. Miguel Fleta, the first Calaf, stands on the steps. (Stuart-Liff Collection)

Conclusion

Casting an overall glance over Puccini's last opera, certain salient points emerge. In a sense there is a paradox about *Turandot*. Although in its technique it belongs very much to the twentieth century, in character and tone it looks back to the nineteenth century. It is the last great romantic opera Italy has produced and perhaps the last Italian opera that enjoys an international success, figuring, more or less regularly, in the repertory of the great opera houses. The Verdi opera with which it can best be compared is *Aida*. Like *Aida*, *Turandot* combines high drama with an impressive stage spectacle in an exotic setting; and like the Verdi work it remains, for all the importance and wealth of orchestral colours, a singers' opera — much in contrast to the 'symphonic' operas of Puccini's German contemporary, Richard Strauss. Its combination of incandescent lyricism with an extraordinary dramatic power has ensured its undiminished success. It also recalls *Tosca* in this and other ways. Thus the heroic portraits of Turandot and Calaf are fore-shadowed to some extent by the lovers of the earlier opera. Both works strictly observe the Aristotelian unities of time, place and action creating in the spectator a subliminal feeling of the utmost concentration and compactness. Again, as in *Tosca*, the action in *Turandot* is set in motion with the rise of the curtain, throwing the spectator *in medias res*, and the plot develops rapidly (in marked contrast to Gozzi's play where the essential action does not really begin until the second act). Moreover, because all Gozzi's quasi-historical allusions are eliminated (as they are to a large extent from Sardou's *La Tosca*) the result is a sense timelessness.

In the last analysis what explains the unique position *Turandot* occupies in Puccini's *oeuvre* and indeed renders it his supreme masterpiece, is the fact that it brings together for the first time the four elements that we find separately in his other operas: the dramatic-heroic (Turandot, Calaf); the lyrical-sentimental (Liù); the comic-grotesque (the Masks); the exotic ambience (a legendary China). It is this synthesis that is responsible for the opera's wider dramatic and emotional range than his other operas. In short, Puccini's swan-song represents his consummation as a musical dramatist.

Puccini's 'Turandot': A Fragment

— studies in Franco Alfano's completion of the score

Jürgen Maehder

'Tutto dipende anche dal materiale, dalle note ed aggiunte lasciati.
Ho letto che c'è quasi tutto!—??—'*
(Letter from Riccardo Schnabl-Rossi to Puccini's son
Antonio, December 5, 1924)

Unfinished works have always fascinated the public, especially since the development of the idea that a musical work is in some sense destined to be finished — *ie* since the Classical Viennese school; and this is true, above all, of compositions left unfinished because of the composer's death. In the case of musical works for the stage, it used to be felt that the dramatic action of an opera deserved to be completed; inviting another composer to finish a score seemed more natural in a musical world where the concept of originality was not as sacrosanct as it is today, and where the score — as was the case with so many 17th-century *pasticci* — was itself sometimes the result of a collaboration between several composers. The case of *Le Duc d'Albe*, for instance, left unfinished by Donizetti in 1839 because of his differences with the director of the Paris Opéra, illustrates this: the necessity of completing the score was not even discussed when, forty years later, Matteo Salvi did so by adding a disproportionate quantity of music of his own invention. It seems that the demands of the drama and the need to supply a dénouement to satisfy the audience overrode any purely musical considerations; only in the 20th century have fragments of opera scores been performed as such — Schoenberg's *Moses und Aaron* or the incomplete version of Alban Berg's *Lulu*.

The question of completing the score of *Turandot*, left unfinished when Puccini died on November 29, 1924, presents a more complex problem than usual for an Italian opera; although still rooted in the mainstream of Italian operatic tradition, *Turandot* closes an era of musical tradition and culture; and although this very tradition of Italian Opera, with its publishers and its impresarios, was to determine the circumstances of the completion of Puccini's score, musical developments had in fact made obsolete many of the traditional conditions in which it was produced. Whereas most unfinished musical works consist of a clearly completed part of the score, some sketches and a large area of transition between both, the circumstances of the creation of *Turandot* almost eliminated any intermediate stage of musical notation. While waiting for the final version of the libretto, Puccini had finished the full score of the first half of Act Three up to the E*b* minor chord on the words 'Liù, poesia'. For the remaining parts of Act Three, Puccini left 23 sheets of musical sketches, partly written on both sides, amounting in total to 36 pages of sketches in short score, with many annotations regarding the

* 'Everything depends also on the material, the notes and so on which are left. I have read that it is almost all there!—??'

orchestration;[1] besides this direct evidence of his musical intentions the composer left valuable written and oral information to his collaborators: to Arturo Toscanini, Giuseppe Adami and Galileo Chini.[2]

Because the first page of the sketches, with Calaf's lines 'Principessa di morte, principessa di gelo . . .' ('Princess of death, princess of frost'), has until now been the only page known to the general public[3] — the love duet and finale of the opera have always been considered as Puccini's own music, with orchestration completed by Franco Alfano (1875-1954). In the course of my research into the orchestration, with a view to a comparative analysis of the organisation of timbres in music of the fin-de-siècle period, I began to study the other sketches left by Puccini; by comparing them to Alfano's score, I discovered that about two-thirds of Alfano's additions must be regarded as his own composition. To appreciate the difficulty of Alfano's task, Puccini's sketches and their musical substance must be described; the problems of transliterating his handwriting and the fragmentary character of the musical notation in these pages make it essential to refer directly to the autograph. Since a critical edition of all the sketches, with transliteration and commentary, is not yet possible, I have chosen here some pages which contain material relevant to the ending of the score as it is now performed, and which give an overall idea of the way Puccini organised his musical material when composing the first draft of a scene which he found extremely difficult to create.

The 23 pages of sketches can be subdivided into four different groups which were originally held together by metal paper-clips; since they have been exposed to humidity — probably by Puccini himself — the clips left traces of rust at the margin of the pages, by means of which it has been possible to reconstruct their original order. Appendix I shows how the sketches follow the chronological order of the action. The first three groups, containing a continuous flow of music, seem to belong to a highly developed stage of composition, whereas the fourth group assembles single pages probably belonging to different stages of the creative process: possibly even some discarded material was conserved in the fourth group because there was some musical idea on the verso of the page which Puccini wanted to keep for a later stage of the composition. The musical textures in the first three groups of sketches are clearly individualised by underlying ideas of rhythmic, harmonic and melodic structure; some of them incorporate musical material taken from a passage in the fourth group. Passages for the transition between the first and the third group of sketches —

[1] These are conserved in the Ricordi archive, Milan. I wish to express my gratitude to G. Ricordi & Co., Milan, for access to their archive; to Mr Carlo Clausetti (Ricordi, Archivio Storico) for precious advice; to Dottoressa Simonetta Puccini, who encouraged my studies from the beginning and followed their progress with vivid interest; to Dr Mosco Carner, who gave valuable advice and encouraged a view of Alfano's first version more orientated towards the problem of dramatic persuasiveness; to Miss Denny Dayviss and Mr Alan Sievewright for having given the first performance of Alfano's original score in modern times; to the 'Schweizerischer Nationalfonds zur Förderung der wissenschaftlichen Forschung' for a fellowship from 1978 to 1979; and to the 'Istituto Storico Germanico' in Rome whose member I have been from 1979 to 1982.

[2] I remember a visit to Comm. Eros Chini†, the son of Galileo Chini, made at Lido di Camaiore (Lucca) in 1982; he remembered how Puccini played the finale of *Turandot* to his father, at that time working on the stage drafts.

[3] Additional pages have been reproduced in the review 'La Scala' (May 1951; December 1958).

Example 1 (page 2 recto)

corresponding to the two bars on page 408 of the current full score — have been sketched out in several different versions; bridging the sections bearing the tempo marks 4/4 and 9/8 must have been a hard task. Unfortunately, there are no passages for the transition from the third to the second group of sketches; this section, the music accompanying Calaf's kiss and Turandot's reaction to it, was left entirely to Alfano's imagination. While reading the following description of some of the more important sketches, it will be helpful to refer to Appendix I, which sets out the interrelationship between Puccini's sketches and the current version of Alfano's score derived from them.[4] Example 1 (page 2 recto) shows Puccini's setting of Turandot's words 'Cosa umana non sono. Son la figlia del cielo, libera e pura. Tu stringi il mio freddo velo, ma . . .' ('I am no human thing. I am the daughter of heaven, free and pure. You clasp my cold veil, but . . .'); the date on the right margin of the page ('vive 10. 10. 24') is the only date on the sketches. The various indications of orchestration have mostly been followed by Alfano; because of Puccini's handwriting, this page caused serious problems of interpretation, especially because the composer did not indicate the exact metrical position of the inserted words 'stringi il mio freddo'.

[4] Studien zum Fragmentcharakter von Giacomo Puccini Turandot, Analecta Musicologica XXII, Laaber 1984; La trasformazione interrotta della principessa, in Atti del primo convegno internazionale sull'opera di Puccini a Torre del Lago, Pisa (Giardini) 1984.

Example 2 (page 5 recto)

Example 2 (page 5 recto), one of the most legible sketches, shows the beginning of the second group, which covers the arioso of the Prince from 'Mio fiore, mio fiore mattutino' ('My flower, my morning flower') until Turandot's words 'La mia gloria è finita' ('My glory has ended'). As can be seen from page 15 recto (here reproduced as example 6), Puccini had previously sketched single elements of the musical texture to be incorporated into the final version of this passage; the two upper staves of example 6 show the word 'fiore', the accompanying chords and the melismatic line of the chorus. The four bars in example 2 are written neatly, almost without correction, showing that the idea of this passage had matured to a state of perfection in the composer's mind. Interestingly, this is borne out by a letter written on May 31, 1924 to his librettist Adami;[5] Puccini mentions that in a further revision of the libretto the words of this duet between Turandot and Calaf have to be conserved, because 'you know that the music already exists'.

The end of this section, Turandot's words 'Che nessun mi veda! La mia gloria è finita!' ('Let no-one see me! My glory has ended!'), is shown by example 3 (page 7 recto of the sketches). The composer's uncertainty as to the continuation of this passage is obvious from his numerous corrections; and, in fact, with the exception of small insertions and of musical citations from previous passages of his work, this passage was to remain the last music by Puccini in the score. The fact that at the stage of sketching the love duet Puccini had had in mind one previously developed passage, Calaf's arioso 'Mio fiore . . .', had caused him to postpone the composition of the preceding lines of the libretto; he returned to them with the third group of sketches, which begins on page 9 recto (example 4). After two bars of the difficult

[5] Puccini, Epistolario, ed. G. Adami, Milano 1928, p. 295.

Example 3 (page 7 recto)

Example 4 (page 9 recto)

Gina Cigna as Turandot. She sang the title role in the first complete recording in 1938. (Stuart-Liff Collection)

bridge section, which were later replaced by another version written down on page 4 recto,[6] Puccini began to compose the lines in which Calaf expresses his desire to Turandot. A previous version of the text of this section has apparently been cancelled; at the second stage the composer added above the stave of Calaf's voice the definitive version of the libretto: 'La tua anima è in alto, ma il tuo corpo è vicino . . .' ('Your soul is on high, but your body is near.'). Although the underlying music is a re-shaping of the introduction to Act Three, Puccini planned a different orchestration, probably because he had to take into account the difficult balance between the orchestral sound and the tenor voice. Agitated demisemiquaver figures were added in the lower register to reflect the great emotional tension of the situation; they counteract the otherwise calm and placid character of the 9/8 movement which vaguely recalls the rhythm of a lullaby. Despite the layer of corrections which covers the whole page, all important elements of the musical texture are already present in abbreviated form; although Alfano did not follow immediately all the verbal indications which Puccini gave for the orchestration, he generally succeeded in the second version of his score to create an orchestral timbre, which — at least within these bars — must be reasonably close to Puccini's intentions.[7]

[6] When preparing the first version of his score, Alfano was unable to decipher the signs by which Puccini suggested the insertion of these two bars; they are missing from it.
[7] The omission of the demi-semi-quavers in Alfano's first version is not due to problems of transliteration; the sketch has been correctly transcribed by Zuccoli.

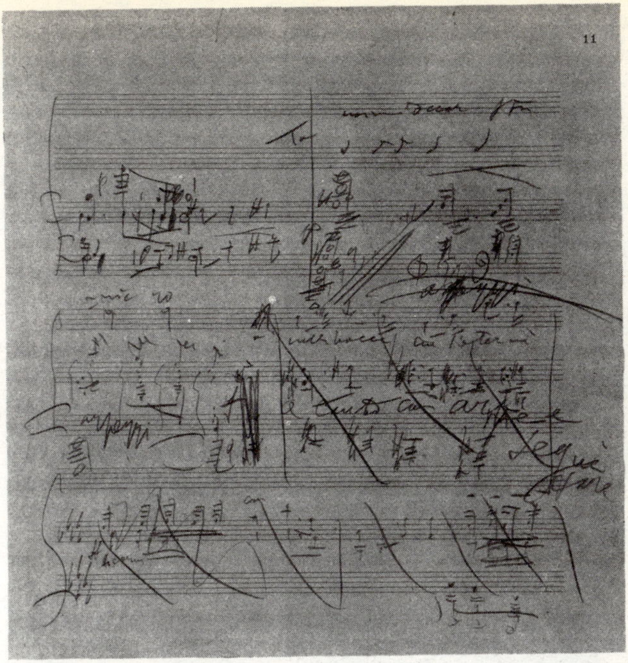

Example 5 (page 11 recto)

The next example, page 11 recto (example 5), is taken from the end of this section; because of a textual error Puccini cancelled the lower half of the page, continuing on page 11 verso with the words 'È un sacrilegio!' ('It is a sacrilege!') which he had forgotten to put to music.

The beginning of the page shows a musical citation from Turandot's Act Two aria; on the two lowest staves Puccini tried to sketch out the presumably definitive version of the music which should have accompanied Calaf's kiss. This moment of the action was to be underlined by a great orchestral *tutti*, based on the lyrical melody derived from Turandot's aria at the centre of Act Two. The fact the Puccini forgot to insert the words 'È un sacrilegio!' made him cancel the whole passage, which then (page 11 verso) acquired a new ending in F major, but without the possibilities suggested by the preceding sketch of continuing the musical line. When completing Puccini's score, Alfano had to invent a different bridge section for Calaf's kiss, and this is the most insensitive and least successful part of his score. There can be little doubt — not only from the evidence of page 11 recto, but also from several single pages within the fourth group of sketches — that Puccini had planned the lyrical outburst of love between Turandot and Calaf in D*b* major; it is therefore hard to understand why Alfano transposed the theme to E*b* minor, confining it to some instruments in the middle range of the orchestra instead of letting it dominate the whole musical texture.[8]

After this bridge section Calaf's arioso had to be inserted (page 5 recto to 7 recto of the sketches); its calm musical character suggests a profound change in the psychological situation of the protagonists, and thus suggests a long

[8] This whole passage has been reduced to a few bars in Alfano's second version; this contributes notably to the impression of psychological incoherence in the principal characters.

Miguel Fleta, the first interpreter of the role of Calaf (Istituto di Studi Pucciniani)

time span in the action between the two groups of sketches. After Turandot's words 'La mia gloria è finita!', the task of creating a continuous musical structure for the rest of the opera passed to Alfano. Besides the enormous problem of reconstructing Puccini's possible intentions for a section of the opera which the composer himself had tried for several years, unsuccessfully, to finish, Alfano's completion was written under the implicit necessity to respect as much as possible the stylistic unity of Puccini's musical idiom. It is highly probable that part of the inherent problem was understood neither by Alfano, nor by the directors of the Ricordi publishing house who had assigned him the task of completing the score — nor by Arturo Toscanini, who had proposed Alfano for the work.

It is well known that the musical world of 19th-century Italy tended to underestimate the importance of orchestration; the composers — who had immense practical skill based on personal experience — simply did not yet need any developed theory of orchestration, while the general public and contemporary musical theory did not realise the increasing importance of attaching an individual orchestral colour to each new work. This is probably the only satisfactory explanation why Alfano, while working to complete the score, did not know Puccini's full score; incredible as this may seem, it is proved by a letter which is preserved in the Ricordi archive.[9] On January 1, 1926, only 17 days before he finally completed his score, Alfano asked

[9] Franco Alfano, letter 134, Ricordi Archive, Milan.

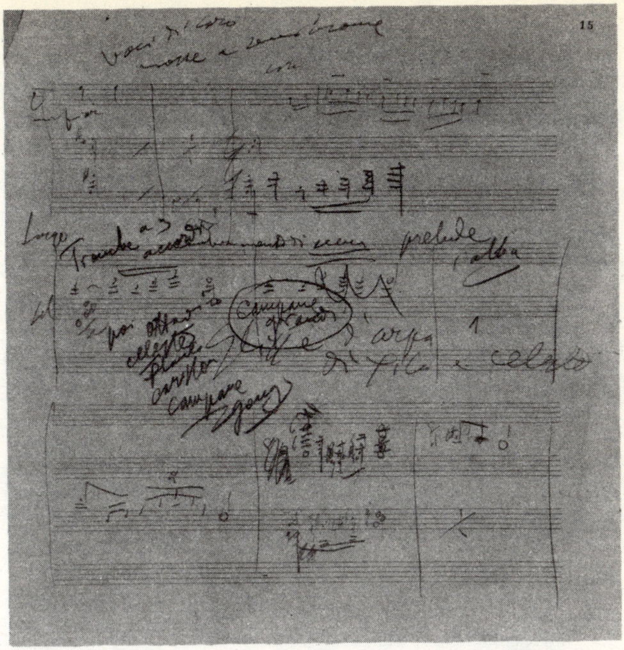

Example 6 (page 15 recto)

Ricordi for a copy of Puccini's full score in order to insert the original orchestration of those passages which he had taken from preceding passages of the opera. It is probably because of this disregard for the orchestration that Alfano stuck so closely to the musical text of Puccini's sketches, but often neglected the verbal indications of orchestration which Puccini gave for the single sketches. This applies especially to the fourth group, running from page 13 recto to page 23 verso; as these were jotted down on single pages and were not ordered chronologically according to the sequence of the action, it must have been very difficult to relate them to the missing parts of the opera. Relying on his sure musical craftmanship Alfano took the motivic elements offered by these sketches as musical raw material, freely changing their patterns of rhythms and intervals and mostly disregarding Puccini's ideas of orchestral timbre. It is very interesting to compare page 15 recto of the sketches (example 6), which on its lower two thirds contains the music that Puccini had planned as an interlude for the stage transformation, to Alfano's elaboration and orchestration of the same motif. Puccini's words read: 'change of scene', 'dawn prelude', 'trumpets and three chords', 'then piccolos, celeste, flute, carillon, bells, 2 gongs'; within the circle he wrote: 'big bells' and underneath: 'Glissandos of harps, xylo[phone] and celeste'. Together with the tempo indication 'Largo' and the few notes of the fanfare-like motif, these words evoke a precise idea of the sound which the composer imagined: a slow, airy 'chinoiserie' composed of notes of short duration, with the solo trumpets entering in chords, not blending at all with heavy brass instruments. Alfano, when using this motivic element in order to construct his interlude on it, conceived an orchestration which is exactly the opposite of Puccini's idea: a post-Wagnerian brass orgy which outdoes all other *tutti* sections of the opera in brutal dynamic force.

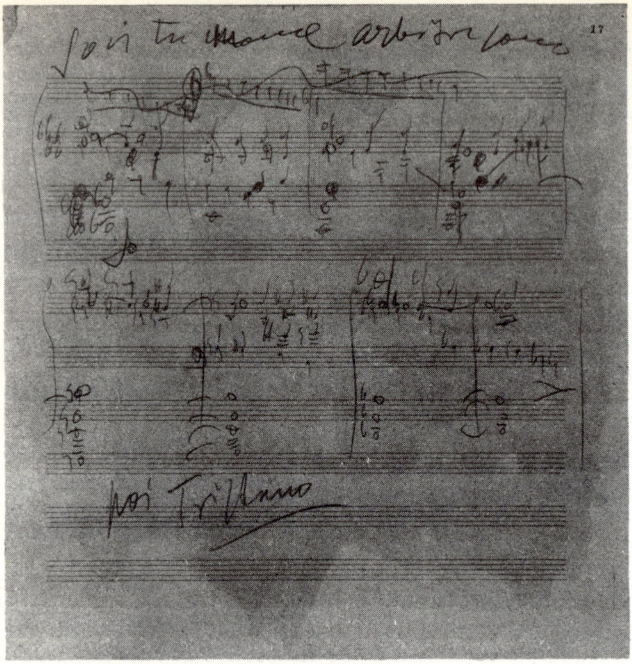

Example 7 (page 17 recto)

Generally speaking, the additions made by Alfano do not attempt to imitate Puccini's musical style. The most obvious differences between Alfano's musical language and Puccini's concern orchestration and the skilful distribution of vocal and orchestral climaxes within a specific period; Alfano's technique of motivic elaboration, although hardly similar to Puccini's style, however, acquires a structural coherence of its own which is not without musical vvalue.

Our knowledge of all the sketches allows us to answer the interesting question whether they contain any relevant musical material that Alfano did not use. When preparing the first — and longer version — of his completion, Alfano discarded only two sketches of usable size, one of which was reintroduced at Toscanini's request into the second version; this was Puccini's music for Calaf's text: 'Il mio mistero? Non ne ho più . . .' ('My mystery? I no longer have any . . .'). The other discarded sketch, a lyrical *tutti* in D*b* major, was originally planned to be the interlude after the disclosure of Calaf's name; this page 17 recto (example 7) was to attract some attention because of Puccini's words 'Poi Tristano' ('Then Tristan') at the bottom of the page. The libretto text on top of the page ('So il tuo nome! Arbitra sono [del tuo destino]' — 'I know your name! I am mistress [of your fate]' includes a fragment from the libretto of Alfano's first version which is never heard in performance, although it still figures in the edition of the libretto. Puccini's allusion to the identity of love and death in his own opera as in Wagner's music drama certainly derives from Calaf's following lines 'Fammi morir!' 'Put me to death!'); with this passage of Alfano's first version, Calaf delivers himself completely to Turandot, and is ready to die for his love.

Although the omission of page 17 recto from Alfano's score must be regarded as a loss in musical substance, the sketch in question represents a type of orchestral texture which Alfano had already proved himself unable to realise at the moment of Calaf's kiss. The difference of generation between Puccini and Alfano and the resulting difference in their compositional technique probably caused a decision against what Puccini intended; the relatively simple pattern of setting for the orchestra (rich-sounding *tutti* throwing the melody in relief, probably given to the violins) could have seemed anachronistic to a composer whose own works of the period show the strong influence of the orchestration of Debussy and Ravel.

If we must regret the omission of page 17 recto from Alfano's score, the question is much more complex for the second passage originally discarded by Alfano, Puccini's setting of the words:

Il mio mistero? Non ne ho piú! Sei mia!	My mystery! I no longer have any! You're mine!
Tu che tremi se ti sfioro,	You who tremble if I touch you!
tu che sbianchi se ti bacio,	You, who pale if I kiss you,
puoi perdermi se vuoi!	can destroy me if you wish!
Il mio nome e la vita insiem ti dono:	I give you together my name and my life:
Io son Calaf il figlio di Timur!	I am Calaf, son of Timur!

Anne Roselle, a very fine German interpreter, who sang the title role at Covent Garden in 1934 and Maria Cebotari, the Bessarabian soprano, as Turandot (Stuart-Liff Collection)

Puccini's corresponding melodic sequence, contained on page 16 recto — and characterised by Spike Hughes as a 'monstrously banal, amateurishly inept sequence'[10] —, would probably not have constituted the final version of this passage; or, if so, it would probably have been rendered more natural by a different surrounding musical structure. But as in this section of the score the responsibility of constructing a coherent musical structure had already passed to Alfano, it does not seem justified to exclude his own, in fact quite beautiful, version of the text. If not superior to the simpler texture of Puccini's setting, it has the major advantage of fitting perfectly into its context. It demonstrates Alfano's sophisticated use of orchestral timbres and reveals the strong influence of Debussy on the interval patterns of his work — a model for this passage could have been the 'Sarabande' of Debussy's suite *Pour le piano* (1901).

In order to reconstruct the genesis of Alfano's score — and to understand some of its incomprehensible shortcomings in orchestral structure — I had planned to compare Alfano's autograph with the first version of the piano reduction, known from Cecil Hopkinson's Puccini bibliography and from Gordon Smith's article in *Opera*.[11] When comparing the microfilm of Alfano's autograph with my copy of the first version in the Ricordi archive in 1978, the Ricordi autograph score proved to be the hitherto unknown full score of Alfano's first version.

From 1978 to 1982, I gradually studied the archive material conserved mostly in Milan in order to reconstruct the genesis of both versions. It was natural to begin by reading Alfano's letters to his editor; a strange change in tone during January 1926 and several allusions to discordant views in the ensuing letters led me to read all the correspondence of the Ricordi company from the date of Puccini's death until the first performance of *Turandot*, i.e. from November 1924 to April/May 1926.[12] The results of these studies can be summarised briefly here, a more detailed study would have to discuss the conflict between the interests of the editor, the interest of Toscanini as conductor of the first performance — and, finally, Alfano's interest, which at that time was limited to ridding himself as quickly as possible of a difficult and controversial task.

Although the first hint at the project of having *Turandot* completed by another composer can be found in a letter written by Puccini's friend Riccardo Schnabl-Rossi only a few days after Puccini's funeral,[13] a decision upon the choice of the person to whom to confide the completion of Puccini's opera was taken only in July 1925; a letter from Alfano to Ricordi, dated 'San Remo, July 5, 1924' is the first evidence that the job was offered to Alfano who did not accept it immediately.[14] On August 25, the contract between Alfano and Ricordi was signed;[15] it is interesting that, although Ricordi had chosen the composer who was to finish the score, the payment of Alfano's fees was entirely supported by Puccini's heirs — with the exception of Alfano's later royalties, which were to be divided equally between the publisher and the heirs. Alfano began work in collaboration with Giuseppe

[10] Spike Hughes, Famous Puccini Operas, London . . .

[11] Cecil Hopkinson, A Bibliography of the works of Giacomo Puccini, New York 1968; Gordon Smith, Alfano and 'Turandot', *Opera*, London 1973.

[12] The correspondence of the Ricordi company was bound in chronological order, forming volumes of 500 pages each; towards the middle of the twenties the correspondence of a year amounts to circa 10 volumes, i.e. 5000 pages.

[13] Giacomo Puccini, Lettere a Riccardo Schnabl, ed. Simonetta Puccini, Milano 1981.

[14] Franco Alfano, letter 126, Ricordi Archive, Milan.

[15] Ricordi, Copialettere, 1925/26-2/292.

Adami; while there is frequent information about meetings between the two men, no similar collaboration seems to have been established between Alfano and Renato Simoni, the other librettist of *Turandot*. Since Alfano suffered from an eye disease which caused a serious delay in his work, Ricordi sent their collaborator Maestro Guido Zuccoli, who had prepared the piano reduction of Puccini's score, to Turin in order to assist Alfano in his work.

When Alfano sent the first pages of the completed piano reduction to Milan, the reaction was not at all positive; the Ricordi archive conserves an offended letter by the composer in which he complains of being constrained to work twice as much as he had planned because of Toscanini's wishes to cut and change his score (January 15, 1926).[16] The answer by Renzo Valcarenghi, at that time commercial director of the company, probably did nothing to calm the artist's offended pride; Alfano was told that the necessity for changes was not to be discussed, and that his request for additional fees was unjustified.[17] A letter by the other general manager of Ricordi, Carlo Clausetti, to Arturo Toscanini, on tour in America at that time, gives a good idea of the actual esteem for Alfano's score and provides us with the only first-hand information that the changes were really demanded by Toscanini:

Maestro Arturo Toscanini — Milan, January 26, 1926
c/o Ricordi & Co.
New York

Dear Maestro,

We are all very happy because of the frequent reports we receive of the marvellous success of your concerts and about this new reassertion of your work as an artist and an Italian.

We wish to inform you that during these days Maestro Alfano has finished and delivered the whole completion of *Turandot*, which has been prepared according to the changes which were decided together with you, and which were explained to him by Mr Adami.

The second section by Puccini ('Che mai osi, straniero') has been put in the right place; another one — which was all stuff invented by Alfano — has been cut and replaced with a short piece based on a theme by Puccini, the aria is now completely new, and is now based in its first section on a motif by Puccini himself ('Del primo pianto, sì, straniero, quando sei giunto') . . . and in the second section on another motif which in Puccini's sketches is in D*b* major . . . etc. . . with a return to the quick tempo of the initial passage.

Finally the *tutti* passages in the finale, which Alfano had assigned to tenor and soprano, have now been given back to the chorus.

I think that we may finally be quite content with the results and I really hope that this will be your impression, too.

Alfano is at the moment working on the orchestration.

With all my best wishes for you, Mrs Carla and Wally, and the same from our friend Valcarenghi.

With a heartfelt handshake from your 'brother'

Carlo Clausetti[18]

Only two days after the date of this letter Alfano informed Ricordi that his score was complete, although on some of the opening pages the relationship between text and music was still unsatisfactory — according to the autograph, this must have been a reference to Calaf's words 'La tua anima è

[16] Franco Alfano, letter 135, Ricordi Archive, Milan.
[17] Ricordi, Copialettere, 1925/26-6/437/438.
[18] Ricordi, Copialettere, 1925/26-7/140/141.

in alto, ma il tuo corpo e vicino . . .'. Because of the extreme haste with which the preparation of the full score and of the material for orchestra and chorus was finished, Alfano had to agree that Adami did these corrections in Milan, without consulting the composer. As copies of telegrams in Ricordi's 'Copialettere' reveal, the offended composer must have felt reluctant to attend the dress rehearsals of his mutilated score; only after the third telegram does he seem to have followed Ricordi's solicitations to participate.[19] When, after the first night of *Turandot*, Ricordi Milan sent telegrams to all their branches in Italy with the text 'Turandot magnifico successo sette chiamate primo atto sei secondo sei terzo' ('Turandot marvellous success, first act seven curtains, second six, third six'), Alfano's score had not yet been performed — Toscanini had finished the opera with Liù's death, pronouncing some words in commemoration of Puccini.

These circumstances of the composition of Alfano's score certainly explain some of its most striking shortcomings — the total lack, for instance, of exotic percussion in the final scene. To obtain a more precise idea of the structural inter-relationship between Alfano's two versions, I have compared both full scores; appendix II, although limited to important cuts and changes, and completely omitting the numerous amendments to the orchestration, gives a vivid picture of the total number of differences. Knowing the time scale under which Alfano had to work, a comparison of his score for *Turandot* with his own operas of the same period seemed to be promising; when studying the score of Alfano's most beautiful opera, *La leggenda di Sakùntala* (Bologna 1921), I found several instances where he re-used motivic elements of his own music, all from Sakùntala's great aria 'Padre! Padre mio santo . . .' in Act Two. Example 8 shows the degree of motivic resemblance. It was natural for Alfano, faced with the necessity of inventing new thematic material for the sections of *Turandot* for which Puccini had not left any sketches, to stick to his own music, and moreover to a score written for a subject with exotic local colour.

A comparison of the two versions reveals that the general lack of coherence in the version currently performed is not due to Alfano's inclusion of his own thematic material but to the numerous cuts which he had to make in his own music. The reduction of his score by 109 bars is the result of 24 different operations, mostly cuts, but also insertions and expansions. The fact that Adami, the librettist, had the task of explaining the necessary cuts to Alfano seems to have had some importance for the musical structure; in fact most of the cuts closely followed the subdivisions of the libretto, but they did not on the whole respect the logic of Alfano's music. The comparison between the two scores reveals moreover that all the cuts were done without resealing the resulting breaks in the musical texture; in short, they were done as if Alfano had used a pair of scissors — without any regard for the development of the different motifs, nor for the inherent distribution of orchestral timbre.

To understand Toscanini's position towards Alfano's score, it must be assumed that the conductor rejected the score submitted by Alfano on the basis of his recollections of how Puccini played the finale to him during Toscanini's visit to Viareggio in October 1924.[20] Although his personal judgement must be accepted, any historical evaluation of the two scores prepared by Alfano must concentrate exclusively on questions of musical structure and dramatic persuasive power. As Mosco Carner has pointed out,

[19] Ricordi, Copialettere, 1925/26-9/456; -9/486; -10/31.
[20] cf. the introduction by Simonetta Puccini to: *Giacomo Puccini, Lettere a Schnabl.*

Example 8. Turandot — the vocal lines from Alfano's completed version. Below: La leggenda di Sakùntala — piano reduction and vocal line of Alfano's own opera. Note the common features, particularly the patterns of sequential development of the motivic material.

TURANDOT
p dolciss.
C'e - ra ne - gli occhi tuo - i la lu - ce de - glie-
SAKUNTALA
poco rit.
a tempo
f
- - ra quan - to a - mor t'ho vo - lu -
poco rit.
a tempo
8va
espressivo
pp
pp
TURANDOT
f
ten.
3
- roi E t'ho o - dia - to per quel - la
SAKUNTALA
più f
poco rit.
- to, quanto a - mo - re ti vo - - - glio
poco rit.
pp

TURANDOT

SAKÙNTALA

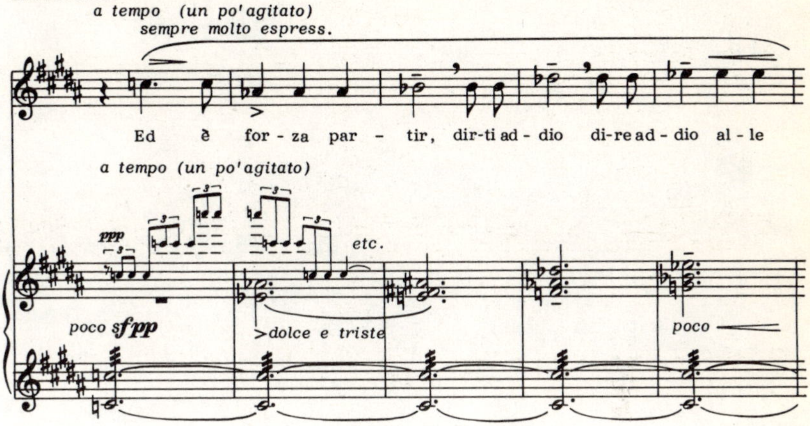

any composer given a task as difficult as the completion of *Turandot* should be given reasonable scope for independent decisions. Appendices I and II demonstrate that the cuts in Alfano's first version were not by any means made to allow a reintegration of large amounts of music by Puccini; the total gain amounts to 23 bars of music derived from his sketches, eleven bars of which were of more or less doubtful quality. The operation forced upon Alfano by Toscanini aimed exclusively at a reduction of the percentage of Alfano's music without offering any alternative solution to the many problems created by the carelessness of his cuts. On the other hand, some changes introduced by Alfano in his second version present a better reading of some of Puccini's most difficult sketches. So the resulting improvement of the musical structure should lead us to prefer a mixed version of Alfano's scores, retaining the best of his interpretations of Puccini's sketches together with his complete music for those passages where Alfano was the sole responsible composer. Such a version can only be prepared on the basis of a critical edition of the whole corpus of musical material left by Puccini and Alfano; while conserving the aesthetic integrity of Alfano's score, it would at last give a final section to the opera which would measure up to its historical importance.

Appendix I

Key to Puccini's sketches

	sketch no.	*corresponds to*	*bar no.*	*discarded*
1st group	1 r		1 - 11	
	1 v		12 - 20	21 - 22
	2 r		21 - 26	27 -28
	2 v	*	28	
	4 r		29 - 30	27 - 28
2nd group	5 r		65 - 68	
	5 v		69 - 72	
	6 r		73 - 76	
	6 v		77 - 82	
	7r		83 - 87	continuation
	7 v	not used (continuation of 7 r)		
	8 r	not used (2 bars D*b* major)		
	8 v	not used (1 bar)		
3rd group	9 r		31 - 34	30
	9 v		35 - 39	
	10 r		40 - 47	
	10 v		48 - 50	
	11 r		51 - 53	3 bars
	11 v		54 - 56	
	12 v	not used (3 bars)		
	13 r	transposed	101 - 105	
	13 v	motif for	210 - 215	
	14 r	not used, text from a preceding version		
	15 r	preparatory sketch for 5 r and 13 v		
	15 v	melody in D*b* major, transformed by Alfano		
	16 r		166 - 176	
	17 r	not used ('So il nome')		
	17 v	not used (melody)		
	18 r	preparatory sketch for 2 r		
	18 v	not used		
	19 r	melody in D*b* major / motif from Calaf's aria		
	20 r	preparatory sketch for 9 r		
	21 r	preparatory sketch for 9 r		
	22 r	not used		
	23 r	musical idea for	251 - 257	
	23 v	not used (two bars of accompaniment)		

* Note: While he was working on the score, Puccini tore page 3 from the manuscript and glued it upside down to page 2 verso.

Appendix II

Synopsis of the two versions of Alfano's score

I. Version	*relationship*	*II. Version*
1 - 19 (Puc)	=	1 - 19 (Puc)
20/21 (Puc)	=	20/21 (Puc)
22	cut	—
23 - 29 (Puc)	similar	22 - 28 (Puc)
—	insertion	29/30 (Puc)
30 - 42 (Puc)	=	31 - 43 (Puc)
43/44	substitution	44 - 47 (Puc)
45/46 (Puc)	similar	48/49 (Puc)
47 - 51	substitution	50 - 55 (Puc)
52/53 (Puc/Alf)	=	56/57 (Puc/Alf)
54 - 69	substitution	58/59
70 - 74	new vocal line	60 -64
75 - 97 (Puc)	=	65 - 87 (Puc)
98 - 110	=	88 - 100
111 - 115 (Puc)	=	101 - 105 (Puc)
116 - 120	=	106 - 110
121 - 124	cut	—
125 - 128	=	111 - 114
129 - 134	new vocal line	115 - 120
135 - 148	cut	—
149 - 168	=	121 - 140
169 - 174	cut	—
175 - 178	=	141 - 144
179 - 182	cut	—
183 - 196	=	145 - 158
—	insertion	159/160
197 - 199	new vocal line	161 - 163
200 - 203	cut	—
204	similar	164
205 - 216	cut	—
217	similar orchestra	165
218 - 226	substitution	166 - 176 (Puc)
227	similar vocal line	177
228 - 257	cut	—
258 - 289	=	178 - 209
290 - 299	=	210 - 219
300 - 324	cut	—
325 - 328	=	220 - 223
329	dilation	224/225
330 - 353	=	226 - 249
354 - 356	identical orchestra	250 - 252
357/358	=	253/254
359 - 361	cut	—
362 - 366	similar	255 - 259
367 - 377	new version	260 - 268

Birgit Nilsson as Turandot, a role she first sang at La Scala in 1958 (Stuart-Liff Collection)

Carlo Gozzi's 'Turandot' and Its Transformation Into Puccini's Libretto

John Black

Puccini's librettists came upon Gozzi's 'Fiaba Cinese teatrale tragicomica', *Turandot*, of 1762 not directly, but through a curious chain of intermediaries. Gozzi's 5-act play was translated into German prose in 1779 by August Clemens Werthes, and this in turn was rewritten by Schiller in verse, for performance in Weimar in 1802. Many years later, in 1863, Andrea Maffei made a word-for-word Italian translation of Schiller's version, and it was this translation that Puccini and his two librettists first consulted. Between play and opera, important changes were introduced into the text, and to see these in perspective, some understanding of the theatrical conditions in which Gozzi was working is necessary.

Carlo Gozzi was born in 1720 into an old and distinguished, but not patrician, Venetian family. His mother was a Tiepolo, and this gave him an entry into aristocratic society. The family had fallen on hard times, and after his brother's unfortunate marriage, Gozzi found himself acquiring first hand experience of lawyers, brokers, money-lenders and the like. Apart from three years military service in Dalmatia, he spent his whole life in Venice, where his well-developed sense of humour, his penetrating observation and descriptive ability were put to literary use. Both by his birth and his artistic leanings he ranged himself with the conservative faction, which was seeking to preserve the older theatrical traditions, and he soon came into conflict with Goldoni, the representative of the 'new look' in the Venetian theatre.

Goldoni's position was diametrically opposed to Gozzi's. He recognized the futility of clinging to traditional forms in the face of the liberalizing influences of the French theatre, particularly the sentimental comedies that were then sweeping across Europe. He set out to write a truly realistic, domestic comedy which was rooted firmly in the day-to-day life of the ordinary people of Venice, portraying the concerns and problems of the people who formed his audience. At the same time he wanted to reform and clean up the old *commedia dell'arte*, which had degenerated into indecent and licentious buffoonery. On this front he attempted to tame the wilder characters by holding them to a written script, thus eliminating the improvisatory element. He was very prolific, and much of his work was of variable quality, but it gained him a popular following. If he was quick to attack the vices and shortcomings of the aristocracy, to glorify the ordinary citizen and to treat the family as the essential structural unit in society, he was also careful not to overstep the mark.

However popular Goldoni's work was with the Venetian theatregoer, it was anathema to the conservative faction, who took the keenest objection to his attacks on the aristocracy, the influence of the sentimental comedies, the emphasis on bourgeois virtues and the careless workmanship which came with prolificacy. While Gozzi shared all these objections of his fellow conservatives, his particular fury was reserved for Goldoni's attacks on the *commedia dell'arte*. He decided to wage the war on Goldoni's own ground, the stage. To this end he embarked on a series of fantastic dramatic 'fables', which could strengthen and develop the *commedia* form, thus providing support for his own favourite troupe of players, and, at the same time fill the theatres.

Octave Dua, William Michael and Parry Jones as Ping, Pang and Pong at Covent Garden in 1929 (Royal Opera House Archives)

The *commedia* had always incorporated unlikely elements of fantasy and improbable coincidences, in the shape of disguises, sleeping-draughts, long lost relatives, kidnapping and the like, as well as the visual and verbal clowning. It was improvised from a 'scenario' (a bare outline of the plot hung up behind the scenes), by actors skilled in repartee and familiar with a wide range of humorous situations and routines of verbal by-play. These actors played in masks, representing well-established comic characters, and an actor's skill consisted in the variations he was able to bring to his interpretation of a stock role. The term 'mask' implies more than the device with which an actor covered his face, and includes the familiar character represented by that device.

Gozzi's purpose was to show that a revitalised *commedia dell'arte* could be successful in theatrical terms. His first 'fable', *L'amore delle tre Melarance* (The Love of Three Oranges) (1759) was a scenario rather than a fully written down play, as the dialogue is only sketched in, but later 'fables' such as *Turandot* (1762) are more completely worked out. They are all fairy tales or similar stories, handled with elaborate devices and full of improbabilities, yet treated with gusto, if (to modern taste) at excessive length. Thus Gozzi the aristocrat and reactionary sought to revive the best in the old forms by emphasizing an escape from reality — the very opposite of what Goldoni stood for. If it was Gozzi who won the battle by driving his rival out of Venice, the theatrical tradition represented by Goldoni was in the long run to win the war.

Interestingly Gozzi's dramatic fables were most appreciated in Germany, where the imaginative elements were seized upon as escapist and in this sense an expression of the romantic. Their potential for operatic treatment was first recognized by E.T.A. Hoffmann, and a number of them have been so used, but none so often as *Turandot*.*

There were at least six operas on this subject in the 19th century from north of the Alps, all probably inspired by Schiller (Blumenroeder, Munich 1810; Reissiger, Dresden 1835; Hoven, Vienna 1839; Løvenskjold, Copenhagen 1854; Konradin, Vienna 1866; Rehbaum, Berlin 1888), as well as Bazzini's *Turanda*, Milan 1867, (important, since Puccini studied with this composer). Other operas on Gozzi subjects included Himmel's *Die Sylphen*, Berlin 1806, and Wagner's *Die Feen*, Munich 1888, both based on *La donna serpente*, and Hartmann's *Ravnen*, Copenhagen 1832, on *Il Corvo*. Then in the twentieth century came an extraordinary recrudescence of interest in the fantastic, and with it Busoni's *Turandot*, Zurich 1917; Prokofiev's *L'amour des trois oranges*, Chicago 1921; Puccini's *Turandot*, Milan 1926; Casella's *La donna serpente*, Rome 1932; and, most recent of all, Henze's *König Hirsch*, Berlin 1956, an opera based on *Il re cervo*.

Turandot was the fable most obviously suited to operatic treatment, since as well as the comic elements in the parts for the Masks, it contains the essence of human conflict, of what might be called sexism, and of the fine dividing line between love and hate. Some of the changes Schiller made when preparing Gozzi's play for the German stage were inevitable, such as the provision of written dialogue for those two of the masks whose parts Gozzi had left in scenario form only. Yet Schiller, by raising the poetic level of Gozzi's language gave a heightened significance to Calaf and Turandot, who are much less exalted people in the original. Puccini's librettists were to give another turn to the screw in raising the two main characters to an even higher plane of existence, worlds away from Gozzi and even from Schiller.

This prompts two questions: how many of Gozzi's original ideas — whether or not filtered through later versions — were carried over into the text which was provided for Puccini; and can the dramatic flaws that are evident in the structure of the libretto (and notably in the last act) be traced back to Gozzi? In preparing the libretto, many of Gozzi's characters had inevitably to be jettisoned, and with them went the involved sub-plot of intrigue which surrounded the discovery of Calaf's identity. Some elements of Gozzi's characters Adelma and Barach were salvaged and used in the new character of Liù. Adelma was a Tartar princess who, in her youth, had taken a special interest in the young prince Calaf, but was now one of Turandot's favourite slaves. Barach had been Calaf's tutor but finding himself in China he had married and settled down. There was in addition a massive condensation of the action. For example, much of the original exposition is reduced to the initial (and new) announcement of the Mandarin at the very beginning of the opera — a masterstroke of introduction which has the effect of making brutally explicit matters which were left more blurred in Gozzi's leisurely introductory dialogue.

The character of the Princess herself is changed more in the transition than is that of Calaf: Gozzi's Turandot is more human, more informal and more confused than is Puccini's, and at no point in the play does she justify her hatred of men by reference to the brutal treatment of an unfortunate ancestress. Psychological credibility was Puccini's aim; as he wrote to Simoni in March, 1920: '. . . a Turandot filtered through a modern brain — yours, Adami's and mine.'

* 'What grandeur, what liveliness and profundity of life dominate in the tales of Gozzi . . . It is not understood why these splendid dramas, in which there are more incisive situations than in many highly praised recent tragedies, have not at least been used with success as opera librettos.' (E.T.A. Hoffmann, *Strange Sufferings of a Theatrical Director*, 1818)

The many explicit, even violent scenes in the opera — the appearance of the executioner and his staff, the grinding of knives, the despairing cries of the doomed prince of Persia, and, particularly, the use of the crowd to raise the dramatic and emotional tension — are all foreign to the spirit of Gozzi, though as elements in a 20th-century opera, especially a Puccinian opera, they are appropriate, even inevitable.

For a long time, Puccini agonised over the basic structure of the opera; should it be cast into two acts or three? The problem did not become urgent

Designs by Franco Zeffirelli for his production at La Scala, 1983 (Archivio Fotografico Teatro alla Scala)

until he was working on the final act, and indeed the difficulties of that act were never properly resolved. It is doubtful if they would have been had Puccini lived to complete it, since to have put the last act right would have involved major surgery elsewhere. The root of the problem is that Puccini's first two acts correspond (closely in their essentials) to Gozzi's first two acts, leaving the final three acts of Gozzi, which are admittedly discursive, to be accounted for in the one final act of the opera. The outline of the plot of the last act had been originally drafted by Puccini as early as 1920, but at that point the problems were not apparent. They loomed larger and larger as flesh was put on the bare outline of the plot.

What did the final act have to cover? Calaf has posed *his* riddle at the end of Act Two (as in Gozzi). Turandot has to learn his name either by intrigue and/or accident (as in Gozzi) or from Calaf himself (as in Puccini). Having found out his name, she could either announce it (as in Gozzi) or keep it to herself. Whatever path she took, a way had to be found to account for her eventual surrender to him, either through Calaf's attempted suicide and her recognition of his steadfastness (as in Gozzi) or through the unexpected and overwhelming physical contact of his kiss (as in Puccini). Thus though the first two acts take over almost exactly the main thrust of Gozzi's play, the mechanics of the plot of Puccini's third act are almost entirely new, and it is in this act that the problems of dramatic structure are greatest.

The first problem concerns Timur and Liù. As a pair, their only effective role is to dissuade Calaf from a course of action which they know can only end in their losing him, whether he wins the Princess or not. When this role is over, Timur is simply overlooked, as if he had never existed. Liù had another role to play, to provide an effective and feminine contrast to the icy Turandot — a role made more necessary by the way in which the Princess had been dehumanised in the opera. Liù's death does not seem to have been envisaged in the early stages of planning, but in November 1922 Puccini wrote to his librettists, 'I think Liù must be sacrificed to some sorrow, but I do not see how to do this unless we make her die under torture. And why not? Her death could help to soften the heart of the Princess.' In other words, Liù had to be removed from the scene, and it would be a pity to waste her departure, which could be used to some dramatic effect, such as an emotional appeal to Turandot.

Far from being softened by Liù's fate, Turandot's only response was to vent her spleen on the unfortunate soldier from whom Liù had snatched a dagger. Turandot had shown some curiosity about Liù when she was alive; dead, Liù was disregarded. All her death achieved was the continuation of a secret which Calaf was himself to reveal. The death of Liù is of course a pitiful moment, and in itself might have made a good curtain; but the opera is about Turandot and Calaf, and Liù is never so incidental as in her death. This, the most moving episode in the opera, disturbs the dramatic balance of the opera and also stands in the way of bringing it to its intended conclusion.

The major dramatic problem was how to turn Turandot's hatred to love. In Gozzi, she is moved by Calaf's fidelity and yields when he attempts suicide. Puccini's instinct told him what was needed in his libretto — Calaf must *kiss* Turandot, a 'kiss of some — long — seconds'. Turandot's hatred may be intellectual, but her love is all too physical and like the Sleeping Beauty she is aroused by a kiss. This crisis is precisely formulated in the lines which were eventually omitted from the ending when it was completed after Puccini's death.

The development of the character of Turandot in the opera is a

Richard Van Allan as the Mandarin at Covent Garden in 1971 (photo: Donald Southern)

remarkable study in sexual psychology. She is obsessed with the story of her ancestress, the princess dragged away and raped by a Tartar king. The echoes of this atavistic experience still resonate in her mind, and have left her both terrified of sexual experience and yet fearfully attracted to it. Consequently she is every bit as vulnerable as is Liù, yet unable by reason of her fear to give simple expression to her feelings in a way such as provides Liù with the solace of loyalty and ultimately the strength of sacrifice. From the moment another Tartar prince comes to China, Turandot knows that her retreat behind an icy wall of rejection cannot be long sustained. She does everything possible to ensure that he does not solve her riddles. After the shock of his first answer she quickly recovers herself, but comes menacingly halfway down the steps in an effort to dominate him. After his second reply, she comes right down to him, and as he falls to his knees she hammers out the third riddle, bending right down over him, her mouth on his face. Neither her icy reserve nor her attempts at intimidation can sway Calaf's single-minded resolve, and she has no defence against someone of whom she is instinctively afraid.

The great duet would be more convincing if, as in Gozzi, there had been some earlier indication of warmth in Turandot's character, but it is at least true to Puccini's own vision of 'two almost superhuman beings descending through love to the level of mankind', as he put it in a letter to Adami just before he died. This descent is of course the greater, the less the initial humanity, and the construction of the first act, in which Turandot appears but does not sing, is designed to portray her as living on a different plane to the rest of humanity. Calaf did not however receive quite the same treatment, and of all Gozzi's main characters he is the least changed. Thus it is where the libretto departs most from the play that it presents the greatest problems. Little wonder if the difficulties inherent in the last act haunted

Puccini, even while he was waiting in Brussels for the operation from which he was never to recover.

No consideration of *Turandot* can overlook the use Puccini and his librettists made of the Masks. Gozzi used four of the traditional figures of the *commedia dell'arte*: Pantalone, who appears as Altoum's secretary; Tartaglia, as Chancellor; Brighella as Master of the Pages; and Truffaldino, as Head of Turandot's eunuchs. The first two of these are provided with written dialogue, and play some direct part in the drama. The latter two remain outside the action, and their scenes are provided in scenario form only, around which they would have woven their familiar verbal routines. All four in Gozzi were unashamedly Venetians, who, finding themselves in China, had found positions for themselves at Court, and they retained their traditional identities.

Not so in the opera. Puccini wanted to retain the masks, to provide the sort of contrast Shakespeare obtained by the juxtaposition of tragic and comic, but he originally had some hesitations about it. They should not be the type of comedian who played to the gallery, he wrote, but rather the clown-philosopher who would contribute occasional well-chosen jokes and opinions. They were to introduce a touch of Italian life and sincerity through their keen observation.

Puccini's librettists reduced the masks from four to three, and shed them of their traditional identities while retaining their functions as Court dignitaries. The resultant trio, renamed Ping, Pong and Pang, are almost entirely undifferentiated, although they are kept sharply in contrast with the rest of the cast. For the most part they keep outside the dramatic action, commenting on it, though they intervene at crucial points, to dissuade Calaf or to tempt him, or to identify Timur and Liù as Calaf's friends. As Chancellor, Grand Purveyor and Chief Cook they are establishment civil servants *par excellence*. If the Prince fails, they are ready for a funeral; if he wins, they have contingency plans for a wedding, too. It is all a great bore; three strokes on the gong, three riddles and it is off with his head. Here they are, stuck in Pekin, heads down in the sacred books, when all they want is to get away to their weekend cottages in the country. If only the Princess would get married and settle down!

The plans for the use of the three Masks matured greatly during the preparation of the opera. Eventually there is nothing left of the *commedia dell'arte*, no occasional jests (except very grim ones), no touches of Italian sincerity. But they do provide a new plane of action and an opportunity for sardonic comment.

They offer an essential contrast to both the vicious turbulence of the crowd and the larger-than-life personalities of the two main characters: Turandot's cold but fearful disdain, which tips over into passion only in response to physical arousal, and Calaf's raw desire which becomes more and more pressing as Turandot seems to withdraw further from him. But their vital contribution to the opera is those periods of repose without which it would not be possible to endure the emotional intensity of the drama.

The libretto is indeed far removed from Gozzi's fussy, ill-organized and prolix play: the various elements are sharply and successfully contrasted, and the use of the Masks, remote as they are from Gozzi's equivalents, shows that the long labour over the text had not been entirely in vain. The tragedy is that so much was left unresolved in the construction of the last act — the disappearance of Timur; the futile and structurally destructive death of Liù and, most serious of all, the failure of the great duet to underwrite the transformation of Turandot herself. Had Puccini lived, the duet would surely have taken a different shape, but it is difficult to envisage changes in the last act sufficient to remove those doubts which cloud a full acceptance of a remarkable text.

The 1939 production at Covent Garden with Eva Turner in the title role (BBC Hulton Picture Library)

Memories of Performing Turandot

Eva Turner DBE

The Lancashire-born and internationally famous soprano Eva Turner DBE made her debut at La Scala singing Freia for Toscanini in 1924 and was present at the world première of 'Turandot' there in 1926. She first sang the title role in Brescia a few months later. It is, perhaps, extraordinary that such a warmly extrovert personality should have become identified with performances of the 'ice-cold princess'. She sang the role many times, in the major Italian theatres and in South America; at Covent Garden in 1937 during the Coronation Season and subsequently in her own final season in 1947.

Before the première of the 1963 production of the opera at Covent Garden, Dame Eva was invited to give a talk about the opera in the Stalls of the Royal Opera House. What follows is an edited transcript of some of the highlights of that unique and memorable evening. When asked how she spent the time before her appearance in the middle of the second act, she later admitted that she used to consider what lay ahead while drinking a small tin of Brands essence of chicken in her dressing room. After that she was 'raring to go'.

The most dramatic part of the opera is the so-called 'Riddle Scene'. I loved posing those riddles: I often wonder if there was a bit of the governess in me! I teach now at the Royal Academy of Music and I find that I am rather governessy, but I hope for the good of the students: I don't like them to be lethargic; I tell them that if they want to sing, they have to be box-office and sell the goods and you'll never do that by being apologetic. You have to have an attitude — as they say in Italy 'l'attitudine e molto importante' — how true! How else are you going to get magnetism across, impinge what you're singing on the ears of the public, and really command them to listen to and enjoy these wonderful operas? How blest we are to have them.

To my students who complain of a headache I say, 'We've no time for headaches, we've too much to do'. The matter of vocal attack in an opera such as *Turandot* is 'molto importante', and so is the approach. Singers must learn that approach and projection are necessary if they are to sing in opera. We cannot impress it on them enough — and no-one can do it for us; *we* have to bring it about.

A singer is responsible for making his own instrument. Whereas an instrumentalist finds the instrument ready, the singer has to put his instrument into action by effecting what we call 'l'impostamento della voce' — the placing of the voice. And when you go to such opera houses as the Teatro San Carlo in Naples, you really are made very much aware of that. If the set for Act Two Scene Two, of *Turandot* is placed so far back that it almost seems to be a theatre in itself, it is difficult to project even as far as the conductor. So where would you be if you couldn't project — where would you be if you didn't have the attitude of delivering the goods? I hope that singers will realise this and not live in a fool's paradise.

When the trumpets sounded the perfect fifths of 'Straniero ascolta' I was always inspired. Many of my students today say they don't want to learn harmony and counterpoint: they only want to sing. I reply that it is essential. 'What are you going to do in the middle of the third act of *Die Walküre* when

Brünnhilde has been thrown down by Wotan ('War es so schmälich'), how are you going to get those notes if you don't know where your roots or inversions are? Nobody in the orchestra will be able to give you a note; you must be sufficient unto yourself. It is therefore your duty to learn harmony and counterpoint, and to practise your piano as a singer.' The Maestro at the Scala said to me when I sang Turandot there, 'Signorina, I will give you the note after the 'Straniero ascolta' when Turandot has to find the pitch for 'nella cupa notte'. 'Give me the note?!' I replied, 'If anyone has to give me that note, I'd be better off as a laundry woman.' Inded they used to have an instrument at the Scala, a sort of pipe, which could give the requisite note — and I'm glad to tell you I never needed it.

As for the lines following 'Padre augusto', I wonder if I used to love singing them so much because they reminded me of the hymns we used to sing in church such as Cwm Rhonda and Aberystwyth.

The third act opens with the beautiful aria 'Nessun dorma'. I have stood in the wings to hear every tenor with whom I have sung this opera, rather than stay in my dressing room. I was always inspired by it.

I have sung the last duet with many and various cuts. I would sometimes arrive for the General Rehearsal (I was often excused from the earlier rehearsals as I had sung the role quite often!) to find that yet another cut had been devised, and the following day was the first performance. Then I would have to take my score to bed with me so that if I woke in the night I could check to see that I had it all right in my mind. You cannot take these things lightly because you must never convey any sense of uncertainty to your public, otherwise your magnetism is destroyed. I was always especially sorry if Turandot's aria 'Del primo pianto' was cut because here all the womanliness in her comes to the fore and the way in which she completely softens and dissolves, conquered by the power of true love, shows the spiritual transformation of Turandot.

In the final scene when I sang the line 'Conosco il nome dello straniero — il suo nome e Amor!' I was always very moved. Although I have never myself married, I find it very wonderful when a woman realises that she has met her affinity.

I knew Maestro Franco Alfano extremely well. He was an opera composer in his own right, and his *Resurrezione* was given at the Teatro Colòn in Buenos Aires in 1927 with Cobelli while I was there. He was, for instance, the Director of the Conservatorio in Turin when I was performing *Fidelio* at the Teatro Regio, and he often came to rehearsals and performances. When I led the company chosen to celebrate the centenary of Simon Bolivàr in Caracas in 1930, he composed a national anthem for Venezuela. The last time I saw him was at Covent Garden in 1947, when he sat in the Royal Box for one of my last performances here as Turandot. When he came to my dressing room afterwards he seemed, I am very glad to say, quite happy about it.

Turandot

An Opera in Three Acts and Five Scenes
by Giacomo Puccini
The last duet and the finale of the opera
were completed by Franco Alfano

Libretto by Giuseppe Adami and Renato Simoni
after the play by Gozzi
English literal translation by William Weaver

Turandot was first performed at the Teatro alla Scala, Milan on April 25, 1926. The first performance in the United States was at the Metropolitan Opera House, New York on November 16, 1926. The first performance in England was at Covent Garden on June 7, 1927.

The Italian text is laid out in verse according to the libretto published by Ricordi in 1926 for the première but it incorporates the word changes which Puccini made as he set the text to music. It includes the complete text of the final scenes — the extra lines in 'Del primo pianto' and the subsequent duet, the dawn chorus and the principals' final exclamations. These were all included in the 1926 libretto although, as the preceding articles have made clear, Alfano's music for them was not performed then. They are marked with an asterisk and square brackets.

The vocal score Ricordi published at the time of the première also included the full Alfano version and this score has been used for the stage directions. These accurately describe the first staging of the opera.

Puccini and his Librettos — An Introductory Note

William Weaver

'I'm writing this in drama class,' Puccini says in a letter to his mother of March 1883, when he was a student at the Milan Conservatory, 'which bores me very much . . .'

Though Puccini was a born opera composer — as even his detractors are forced to admit — he was not a born man of the theatre; and though he spent a great deal of his time going to plays in his mature years, he had no well-defined literary tastes. One might almost say of him that he not only didn't know much about art, he didn't even know what he liked. In fact, the story of the librettos he *almost* set would be much longer — and even more tormented — than the toilsome story of the selection and composition of his dozen operas. Through most of these operas a linking thread can be traced: the pathetic Anna of *Le Villi*, Puccini's first work for the theatre, is, as a character, strikingly similar to the poor slave girl Liù of the posthumous *Turandot*.

The fact is that Puccini, unlike his contemporaries Mascagni and Leoncavallo, for example, knew the nature of his talent, its special qualities and its limitations. At times he toyed with grand themes (for years he dreamed, off and on, of a *Marie Antoinette*); he thought of Shakespeare and of Victor Hugo, but in the end he returned to more congenial if less illustrious authors.

Like Verdi, Puccini drove his librettists crazy. Even when he was hardly more than a student and writing his first opera, he wrote to his librettist, Ferdinando Fontana, asking him to make changes in the text. Fontana, several years older than Puccini and already a fairly well-established writer and theatrical figure, was reluctant to make them. Later, when Puccini himself was established, he made his writers revise and recast whole librettos three or four times, and the process continued even after the works had been performed.

But if one reads the correspondence between Verdi and his 'poets' and the correspondence between Puccini and his, the differences between the two composers' characters become obvious. Verdi made demands based on his inner certainty of what he wanted. Puccini, a weaker man, had to try things first this way, then that, until he gradually gained confidence in what he was doing. Another evidence of his insecurity is the fact that he most frequently tended to choose for his subjects plays that were already big hits on the legitimate stage (like *Tosca*, *Madame Butterfly*, *The Girl of the Golden West*) or subjects that other composers had set (*Manon Lescaut*) or wanted to set (*La Bohème*).

In Verdi's day the librettist was often a mere theatre employee; one ordered so many pages of drama from him as one ordered so many costumes from the dressmaker. By the last years of Verdi's career (which coincide with the beginning of Puccini's) this was all changed. Creeping Wagnerism and increased sophistication in musical circles had made the librettist a respectable figure. From Fontana on, Puccini dealt with esteemed men-of-letters, editors of literary journals, successful playwrights. Read nowadays, the librettos, as examples of Italian poetry, are not really so superior to the much-maligned texts of Verdi's Francesco Maria Piave and Antonio Somma. At best, Puccini's librettos have a quaint turn-of-the-century, *art nouveau* flavour. But, as the librettist Luigi Illica wrote to Puccini's publisher and mentor Giulio Ricordi: 'I still remain of my opinion: the form of a libretto is made by the music, and nothing but the music; it alone . . . is the form! A libretto is merely the outline. And Méry [French librettist of, among other things, Verdi's *Don Carlos*] is right when he says: "Verses in operas are written only for the convenience of the deaf . . ." '

In the end the important thing about the librettos of Giacosa and Illica, Adami, Forzano — like those of Piave and Cammarano — is that they inspired the composer to write great operas.

The libretto of *Turandot* was born in a burst of enthusiasm around a luncheon table in Milan in the summer of 1920. Seated at it were Puccini, his younger friend Giuseppe Adami (librettist of *La rondine* and *Il tabarro*), and the distinguished dramatist and critic Renato Simoni, who had recently collected into a volume the accounts of his travels in the Orient. The two writers were put to work at once; but even their distinction and their considerable theatrical experience did not save them from Puccini's constant demands for revision. Had Puccini not died before the opera's completion, he would probably have insisted on still further changes. Still, Adami and Simoni managed to give him one of his most haunting and colourful texts, unconventional in its dramatic structure and unusual in its mixture of passion and pathos with irony, an infrequent but welcome ingredient in Puccini's operas.

The following translation was meant simply as a guide to that Italian text, and therefore has absolutely no literary pretensions. On the contrary, the translator has deliberately — and with difficulty — resisted all temptation to prettify the English at the expense of literal, even if quaint or gawky, fidelity to Adami's and Simoni's original words.

CHARACTERS

The Princess Turandot	*soprano*
The Emperor Altoum	*bass*
Timur *exiled Tartar king*	*bass*
The Unknown Prince (Calaf) *his son*	*tenor*
Liù *a young slave girl*	*soprano*
Ping *Grand Chancellor*	*baritone*
Pang *Grand Purveyor*	*tenor*
Pong *Grand Cook*	*tenor*
A Mandarin	*baritone*
The Prince of Persia	—
The Executioner	—

Imperial Guards, the Servants of the Executioner, Boys, Priests, Mandarins, Dignitaries, Eight Sages, Turandot's Handmaidens, Soldiers, Standard-bearers, Musicians, the Ghosts of the Dead, the Crowd.

In Peking, in legendary times.

Franco Zeffirelli's design for Act One in his 1983 production at La Scala (Archivio Fotografico Teatro alla Scala)

Act One

The walls of the great Violet City: the Imperial City. The massive ramparts enclose almost the whole stage in a semi-circle. Their movement is broken only on the right by a great loggia, all sculptured and carved with monsters, unicorns and phoenixes, its columns supported by the backs of massive tortoises. At the foot of the loggia, held up by two arches, is a gong of very sonorous bronze.

Some poles are set in the ramparts which bear the skulls of the executed. At left and in the background three gigantic gates open in the walls. When the curtain goes up we are in the most dazzling hour of sunset. Peking, which slopes away in the distance, sparkles, golden.

The square is filled with a picturesque Chinese crowd, motionless, listening to the words of a mandarin. From the top of the rampart, where the red and black Tartar guards flank him, he reads a tragic decree.

MANDARIN

People of Peking!	Popolo di Pekino!
This is the law: Turandot, the Pure,	La legge è questa: Turandot, la Pura,
will be the bride of the man, of royal blood,	sposa sarà di chi, di sangue regio,
who solves the three riddles that she will propose.	spieghi i tre enigmi ch'ella proporrà.
But he who faces the trial and remains defeated,	Ma chi affronta il cimento e vinto resta,
must offer his haughty head to the axe.	porga alla scure la superba testa.

THE CROWD

Ah! Ah!	Ah! Ah!

MANDARIN

The Prince of Persia	Il Principe di Persia
had luck against him:	avversa ebbe fortuna:
at the rise of the moon,	al sorger della luna,
by the executioner's hand	per man del boia
let him die!	muoia!

The mandarin retires and the crowd becomes increasingly restive with mounting tumult.

THE CROWD

Let him die! Yes, let him die!	Muoia! Si, muoia!
We want the executioner!	Noi vogliamo il carnefice!
Quickly, quickly! Let him die, die!	Presto, presto! Muoia! muoia!
To the torture! Let him die, die!	Al supplizio! Muoia! muoia!
Quickly, quickly!	Presto, presto!
If you don't appear, we'll waken you!	Se non appari, noi ti sveglierem!
Pu-Tin-Pao! Pu-Tin-Pao! Pu-Tin-Pao!	Pu-Tin-Pao! Pu-Tin-Pao! Pu-Tin-Pao!

(*and, trying to broach the rampart*)

To the palace! To the palace! To the palace!	Alla reggia! Alla reggia! Alla reggia!

The guards thrust back the crowd. In the shoving many people fall. Confused voices of frightened people. Shouts. Protests. Invocations.

THE GUARDS

Back, dogs! Back, dogs!	Indietro, cani! Indietro, cani!

THE CROWD

Oh, cruel ones! Stop, for heaven's sake!	Oh, crudeli! Pel cielo, fermi!
Oh, my mother! Ahi! My babies!	O madre mia! Ahi! I miei bimbi!

THE GUARDS

Back, dogs!	Indietro, cani!

LIÙ
(*desperately*)

My old one has fallen!	Il mio vecchio è caduto!

THE CROWD

Cruel ones! Be human! Don't hurt us!	Crudeli! Siate umani! Non fateci male!

LIÙ

Who will help me? Who will help me lift him up? My old one has fallen . . . Pity, pity . . . !	Chi m'aiuta? Chi m'aiuta a sorreggerlo? Il mio vecchio è caduto . . . Pietà, pietà!

And she casts an imploring glance around. Suddenly a young man runs up, bends over the old man, and bursts out with a cry.

THE UNKNOWN PRINCE

Father! My father!	Padre! Mio padre!

THE GUARDS

Back!	Indietro!

THE UNKNOWN PRINCE

Oh, father, yes, I find you again!	O padre, si, ti ritrovo!

THE CROWD

Cruel ones!	Crudeli!

THE UNKNOWN PRINCE

Look at me! It isn't a dream!	Guardami! Non è sogno!

THE CROWD

Why are you striking us? Alas! Pity! Pity!	Perchè ci battete? ahimè! Pietà! Pietà!

LIÙ

My lord!	Mio signore!

THE UNKNOWN PRINCE
(*with mounting anguish and emotion*)

Father! Listen to me! Father . . . ! It is I! And blessed be grief for this joy that a pitying God gives us.	Padre! Ascoltami! Padre . . . ! Son io! . . . E benedetto sia il dolor per questa gioia che ci dona un Dio pietoso.

TIMUR
(*coming to, opens his eyes, stares at his saviour, almost doesn't believe the reality, cries to him:*)

Oh, my son! You! Alive?	O mio figlio! tu! vivo?!

THE UNKNOWN PRINCE
(*with terror*)

Be silent!	Taci!

(*and, assisted by Liù, drawing Timur to one side, still bent over him, in a broken voice, with caresses, with tears:*)

He who usurped your crown is seeking me and pursuing you! There is no refuge for us, father, in the world!	Chi usurpò la tua corona me cerca e te persegue! Non c'è asilo per noi, padre, nel mondo!

TIMUR

I sought you, my son, and I believed you dead!	T'ho cercato, mio figlio, e t'ho creduto morto!

THE UNKNOWN PRINCE

I wept for you, father . . . and I kiss these sainted hands!	T'ho pianto, padre . . . e bacio queste mani sante!

TIMUR

Oh, son, found again!	O figlio ritrovato . . . !

THE CROWD

(*which has gathered in the meanwhile near the ramparts, now emits a cry of fierce intoxication*)

Here are the executioner's servants! Let him die! Die! Die! Die!	Ecco i servi del boia! Muoia! Muoia! Muoia! Muoia!

In fact, at the top of the walls, dressed in lurid, bloodstained rags, there appear, grotesquely tragic, the executioner's servants, dragging the enormous sword, which they sharpen on an immense whetstone.

TIMUR

(*still on the ground, to his son bent over him, in a low voice*)

The battle lost, an old king without kingdom and in flight, I heard a voice that said to me: 'Come with me, I'll be your guide . . .' It was Liù!	Perduta la battaglia, vecchio re senza regno e fuggente, una voce sentii che mi diceva: 'Vien con me, sarò tua guida . . .' Era Liù!

THE UNKNOWN PRINCE

Bless her!	Sia benedetta!

TIMUR

And I would fall, exhausted, and she would dry my tears, she begged for me . . .	Ed io cadeva affranto, e m'asciugava il pianto, mendicava per me . . .

THE UNKNOWN PRINCE

(*staring at the girl, moved*)

Liù . . . who are you?	Liù . . . chi sei?

LIÙ

(*humbly*)

I am nothing . . . a slave, my lord . . .	Nulla sono . . . una schiava, mio Signore . . .

THE CROWD

Turn the whetstone! Turn the whetstone!	Gira la cote! Gira la cote!

THE UNKNOWN PRINCE

And why have you shared such anguish?	E perchè tanta angoscia hai diviso?

LIÙ

(*with ecstatic sweetness*)

Because one day . . . in the Palace, you smiled at me.	Perchè un dì . . . nella Reggia, mi hai sorriso.

THE CROWD

(*inciting the executioner's servants*)

Turn the whetstone! Turn!	Gira la cote! Gira!

Then two servants, who have cleaned the blade, make it pass and clank on the whetstone which turns dizzyingly. Sparks fly, and the work becomes fiercely animated, accompanied by a raucous song which the crowd echoes.

THE EXECUTIONER'S SERVANTS

(*savagely*)

Oil! Sharpen! Let the blade flash, spurt fire and blood! Work never languishes, never languishes . . .	Ungi! Arrota! Che la lama guizzi, sprizzi fuoco e sangue! Il lavoro mai non langue, mai non langue . . .

THE CROWD

Never languishes . . .	Mai non langue . . .

THE EXECUTIONER'S SERVANTS

. . . where reigns, where reigns Turandot!	. . . dove regna, dove regna Turandot!

THE CROWD

. . . where reigns Turandot!	. . . dove regna Turandot!

THE EXECUTIONER'S SERVANTS

Oil! Sharpen!	Ungi! Arrota!

ALL

Fire and blood!	Fuoco e sangue!

THE CROWD

Forward, forward, sweet lovers!	Dolci amanti, avanti, avanti!

THE EXECUTIONER'S SERVANTS

With hooks and with knives we are ready to embroider your skins!	Cogli uncini e coi coltelli noi siam pronti a ricamar le vostre pelli!

THE CROWD

Sweet lovers, forward, forward! He who will strike that gong will see her appear!	Dolci amanti, avanti, avanti! Chi quel gong percuoterà, apparire la vedrà!

THE EXECUTIONER'S SERVANTS

He will see her appear, white as jade . . .	Apparire la vedrà, bianca al pari della giada . . .

ALL

Cold as that sword . . .	Fredda come quella spada . . .

THE EXECUTIONER'S SERVANTS

. . . is the beautiful Turandot!	. . . è la bella Turandot!

THE CROWD

Is the beautiful Turandot! Sweet lovers, forward, forward! When the gong clangs the executioner rejoices! Love is vain if there is no luck! The riddles are three, death is one! Yes, the riddles are three, death is one! Who will strike that gong?	È la bella Turandot! Dolci amanti, avanti, avanti! Quando rangola il gong gongola il boia! Vano è l'amore se non c'è fortuna! Gli enigmi sono tre, la morte è una! Si, gli enigmi sono tre, la morte è una! Chi quel gong percuoterà?

THE EXECUTIONER'S SERVANTS

When the gong clangs the executioner rejoices. Oil! Sharpen! Death is one!	Quando rangola il gong gongola il boia. Ungi! Arrota! La morte è una!

ALL

Oil! Sharpen! Let the blade flash, spurt fire and blood! Work never languishes where reigns Turandot! Ah!	Ungi! Arrota! Che la lama guizzi, sprizzi fuoco e sangue! Il lavoro mai non langue dove regna Turandot! Ah!

As the servants go off to take the sword to the executioner, the crowd forms picturesque groups here and there on the ramparts and with fierce impatience examines the sky, which little by little has grown dark.

THE CROWD

Why does the moon delay? Wan face, show yourself in the sky! Quickly! Come! Rise! O severed head! O bleak one! Come! Rise! Show yourself in the sky! O severed head! O bloodless one! O bloodless, o bleak!	Perchè tarda la luna? Faccia pallida, mostrati in cielo! Presto! Vieni! Spunta! O testa mozza! O squallida! Vieni! Spunta! Mostrati in cielo! O testa mozza! O esangue! O esangue, o squallida!

O taciturn!
O pale lover of the dead!
How the cemeteries await your funereal light!
O bloodless, o bleak!
O severed head!

O taciturna!
O amante smunta dei morti!
Come aspettano il tuo funereo lume i cimiteri!
O esangue, o squallida!
O testa mozza!

(and, as little by little a lunar light spreads)

There's a glimmer down there!
Come, quickly! Rise!
There's a glimmer down there,
which spreads in the sky its pallid light!
Pu-Tin-Pao! The moon has risen!
Pu-Tin-Pao! Pu-Tin-Pao!

Ecco laggiù un barlume!
Vieni, presto, spunta!
Ecco laggiù un barlume,
dilaga in cielo la sua luce smorta!
Pu-Tin-Pao! La luna è sorta!
Pu-Tin-Pao! Pu-Tin-Pao!

The gold of the background has changed into a livid silver colour. The icy whiteness of the moon spreads over the ramparts and over the city. At the gate in the walls the guards appear, dressed in long black tunics. A lugubrious dirge spreads. The procession advances, preceded by a group of boys who sing:

THE BOYS

There, on the mountains of the East,
the stork sang.
But April did not reflower,
but the snow did not thaw.
From the desert to the sea — don't you hear
a thousand voices sigh:
'Princess, come down to me!
Everything will bloom,
everything will shine! Ah!'

Là sui monti dell'Est
la cicogna cantò.
Ma l'april non rifiorì,
ma la neve non sgelò.
Dal deserto al mar — non odi tu
mille voci sospirar:
'Principessa, scendi a me!
Tutto fiorirà,
tutto splenderà! Ah!'

The executioner's servants advance, followed by the priests who carry the funeral offering. Then the mandarins and the high dignitaries. And finally, very handsome, almost childish, appears the young Prince of Persia. At the sight of the victim, who comes forward, dazed, dreaming, his white neck bared, his gaze absent, the crowd's ferocity is changed into ineffable pity. When the young Prince of Persia is on the stage, there appears, enormous, gigantic, tragic, the executioner, carrying his immense sword on his shoulder.

THE CROWD

O youth!
Mercy!
Mercy!
How steady is his step! Mercy!
How sweet, how sweet is his face!
He has intoxication in his eyes! Pity!
He has joy in his eyes!
Ah! Mercy!
Pity on him! Princess!
Pity!
Mercy!
Pity on him, pity, pity!

O giovinetto!
Grazia!
Grazia!
Com'è fermo il suo passo! Grazia!
Com'è dolce, come è dolce il suo volto!
Ha negli occhi l'ebbrezza! Pietà!
Ha negli occhi la gioia!
Ah! la grazia!
Pietà di lui! Principessa!
Pietà!
Grazia!
Pietà di lui, pietà, pietà!

THE UNKNOWN PRINCE

Ah! Mercy!
Let me see you ~~and let me curse you!~~
Cruel one, let me curse you!

Ah! la grazia!
Ch'io ti veda e ch'io ti maledica!
Crudele, ch'io ti maledica!

But the cry breaks off on his lips, because, from the height of the imperial balcony, Turandot shows herself. A ray of moonlight illuminates her. The Princess seems almost incorporeal, like a vision. Her masterful attitude and her haughty gaze make the tumult cease magically. The crowd prostrates itself, faces to the ground. Only the Prince of Persia, the executioner and the Unknown Prince remain standing.

THE UNKNOWN PRINCE

O divine beauty, o wonder!
O dream, o divine beauty, o wonder!

O divina bellezza, o meraviglia!
O sogno, o divina bellezza, o meraviglia!

And he covers his face with his hands, dazzled. Turandot makes an imperious gesture: it is the death sentence. The executioner bows his head, assenting. The lugubrious dirge resumes. The procession moves, climbs the walls, disappears beyond the ramparts, and the crowd follows it.

THE WHITE PRIESTS OF THE PROCESSION

O great Kung-tze! May the spirit of the dying man come to you!	O gran Koung-tzè! Che lo spirto del morente giunga fino a te!

Their voices die away. Turandot is no longer there. In the half light of the deserted square only Timur, Liù and the Unknown Prince remain. The Prince is still motionless, ecstatic, as if the unexpected vision of beauty had fatally riveted him to his destiny. Timur approaches him, calls him, stirs him.

TIMUR

Son! What are you doing?	Figlio! Che fai?

THE UNKNOWN PRINCE

Don't you feel it? Her fragrance is in the air! It's in my soul!	Non senti? Il suo profumo è nell'aria! è nell'anima!

TIMUR

You are lost!	Ti perdi!

THE UNKNWON PRINCE

O divine beauty, o wonder! I suffer, father, suffer!	O divina bellezza, o meraviglia! Io soffro, padre, soffro!

TIMUR

No! No! Cling to me! Liù, you speak to him! There's no safety here! Take his hand in your hand!	No! No! Stringiti a me! Liù, parlagli tu! Qui salvezza non c'è! Prendi nella tua mano la sua mano!

LIÙ

Lord! Let us go far away!	Signore! Andiam lontano!

TIMUR

Life is down there!	La vita c'è laggiù!

THE UNKNOWN PRINCE

This is life, father!	Quest'è la vita, padre!

TIMUR

Life is down there!	La vita c'è laggiù!

THE UNKNOWN PRINCE

I suffer, father, suffer!	Io soffro, padre, soffro!

TIMUR

There's no safety here!	Qui salvezza non c'è!

THE UNKNOWN PRINCE

Life, father, is here!	La vita, padre, è qui!

(*freeing himself, he rushes toward the gong, which glows with a mysterious light, and shouts:*)

Turandot! Turandot! Turandot!	Turandot! Turandot! Turandot!

THE PRINCE OF PERSIA
(*within, as if in supreme invocation*)

Turandot!	Turandot!

Then, the shout of the crowd, rapid and violent as a burst of flame:

THE CROWD

Ah!	Ah!

TIMUR

You wish to die thus? | Vuoi morire così?

THE UNKNOWN PRINCE

To conquer, father,
in her beauty! | Vincere, padre,
nella sua bellezza!

TIMUR

You wish to end thus? | Vuoi finire così?

THE UNKNOWN PRINCE

To conquer gloriously in her beauty! | Vincere gloriosamente nella sua bellezza!

And he rushes toward the gong. But suddenly, between them and the luminous disk, three mysterious figures place themselves. They are Ping, Pang, Pong, three grotesque Masks, the Emperor's three ministers, respectively: the Grand Chancellor, the Grand Purveyor, the Grand Cook. The Unknown Prince steps back. Timur and Liù huddle together, fearfully, in the shadow. The gong has become dark.

THE MINISTERS
(*pursuing and surrounding the Prince*)

Stand still! What are you doing? Stop! Who are you? What are you doing? What do you want? Go away! Go, this is the gate to the great butcher's shop! Madman, go away!	Fermo! Che fai? T'arresta! Chi sei? Che fai? Che vuoi? Va' via! Va', la porta è questa della gran beccheria! Pazzo, va' via!

PING

Here they garrotte you! | Qui si strozza!

PONG AND PANG

They impale you! | Si trivella!

PING

They cut your throat! | Si sgozza!

PONG AND PANG

They skin you alive! | Si spella!

PING

They sink hooks into you and behead you! | Si uncina e scapitozza!

PONG AND PANG

Go away! | Va' via!

PING

They saw you up and disembowel you! Promptly, hastily go back to your country to look for a doorpost to break your head on! But not here!	Si sega e si sbudella! Sollecito, precipite, al tuo paese torna in cerca d'uno stipite per romperti le corna! Ma qui no!

PONG AND PANG

Go away! Go back to your country! What do you want? Who are you? Go away! Go away!	Va' via! Al tuo paese torna! Che vuoi? Chi sei? Va' via! Va' via!

THE MINISTERS

But not here! Madman, go away! Go away!	Ma qui no! Pazzo, va' via! va' via!

THE UNKNOWN PRINCE
(*with vehemence*)

Let me pass!	Lasciatemi passare!

(*The ministers block his way.*)

PONG

Here all the cemeteries are occupied!	Qui tutti i cimiteri sono occupati!

PANG

Here the native madmen suffice!	Qui bastano i pazzi indigeni!

PING

We don't want any more foreign madmen!	Non vogliam più pazzi forestieri!

PONG AND PANG

Either you flee, or your funeral is drawing near!	O scappi, o il funeral per te s'appressa!

THE UNKNOWN PRINCE
(*with mounting vigour*)

Let me pass!	Lasciatemi passar!

PONG AND PANG

For a princess! Phew!	Per una Principessa! Peuh!

PONG

What is she?	Che cos'è?

PANG

A female with a crown on her head!	Una femmina colla corona in testa!

PONG

And a cloak with fringe!	E il manto colla frangia!

PING

But if you strip her naked . . .	Ma se la spogli nuda . . .

PONG

. . . she's flesh!	. . . è carne!

PANG

She's raw flesh!	È carne cruda!

THE MINISTERS

It's inedible stuff! Ha! Ha! Ha!	È roba che non si mangia! Ah, ah, ah!

THE UNKNOWN PRINCE

Let me pass! Let me go!	Lasciatemi passare! Lasciatemi!

PING
(*with comic calm and dignity*)

Give up women! Or take a hundred brides, for, after all, the most sublime Turandot in the world has a face — two arms — and two legs — yes — beautiful, imperial ones — yes, yes, beautiful, yes — but still legs! With a hundred wives, oh foolish man, you'll still have a surplus of legs!	Lascia le donne! O prendi cento spose, che, in fondo, la più sublime Turandot del mondo ha una faccia — due braccia — e due gambe — si — belle, imperiali — si, si, belle, si — ma sempre quelle! Con cento mogli, o sciocco, avrai gambe a ribocco!

Two hundred arms! And a hundred soft bosoms | Duecento braccia! E cento dolci petti
scattered in a hundred beds! | sparsi per cento letti!

PONG AND PANG

A hundred bosoms . . . | Cento petti . . .

THE MINISTERS

. . . in a hundred beds! Ha! ha! ha! | . . . per cento letti! Ah, ah, ah!
(*and they snicker, pressing closer and closer to the Prince*)

THE UNKNOWN PRINCE
(*with violence*)

Let me pass! | Lasciatemi passar!

THE MINISTERS

Madman, go away! | Pazzo, va' via!

Some maidens dressed in white — Turandot's handmaidens — look over the balustrade of the imperial balcony and, whispering, they admonish:

TURANDOT'S HANDMAIDENS

Silence! Hola! | Silenzio, olà!
Who's talking down there? | Laggiù chi parla?
Silence! Silence! | Silenzio! Silenzio!
It is | È l'ora
the very sweet hour of sleep! | dolcissima del sonno!
Sleep is grazing | Il sonno sfiora
Turandot's eyes! | gli occhi di Turandot!
The darkness is scented with her perfume! | Si profuma di lei l'oscurità!

PING

Away from there, chattering females! | Via di là, femmine ciarliere!

THE MINISTERS

Away from there! | Via di là!
(*with sudden concern, because they realize that they have left the Prince free for a moment*)
Watch out for the gong! | Attenti al gong!
Watch out for the gong! | Attenti al gong!

The handmaidens have vanished. The Prince, absently, repeats:

THE UNKNOWN PRINCE

The darkness is scented with her perfume! | Si profuma di lei l'oscurità!

PANG

Look at him, Pong! | Guardalo, Pong!

PONG

Look at him, Ping! | Guardalo, Ping!

PING

Look at him, Pang! | Guardalo, Pang!

PANG

He's deafened! | È insordito!

PONG

Stunned! | Intontito!

PING

Dazzled! | Allucinato!

TIMUR
(*aside to Liù*)

He's no longer listening to them, alas! | Più non li ascolta, ahimè!

THE MINISTERS
(*determined*)

Come! Let us speak to him, all three together! | Su! Parliamogli in tre!

They gather around the Prince in grotesque poses.

PANG

Night without a little lamp . . . | Notte senza lumicino . . .

PONG

. . . black flue of a chimney . . . | . . . gola nera d'un camino . . .

PING

. . . are clearer than Turandot's riddles! | . . . son più chiare degli enigmi di Turandot!

PANG

Iron, bronze, wall, rock . . . | Ferro, bronzo, muro, roccia . . .

PONG

. . . your stubborn head . . . | . . . l'ostinata tua capoccia . . .

PING

. . . are less hard than Turandot's riddles! | . . . son men duri degli enigmi di Turandot!

PANG

So go! Say good-bye to all! | Dunque va'! Saluta tutti!

PONG

Cross the mountains, ford the streams! | Varca i monti, taglia i flutti!

PING

Keep clear of Turandot's riddles! | Sta alla larga dagli enigmi di Turandot!

The Prince has almost no strength to react any longer. But then vague calls, not voices but shadows of voices, spread out from the darkness of the ramparts. And here and there, barely perceptible at first, then gradually more livid and phosphorescent, the ghosts appear. They are those who were in love with Turandot and who, defeated in the tragic trial, have lost their lives.

THE VOICES OF THE SHADOWS

Don't delay!
If you call, she appears,
who makes us, dead men, dream!
Make her speak!
Make us hear her!
I love her!
I love her!
I love her!

Non indugiare!
Se chiami, appare
quella che, estinti, ci fa sognare!
Fa' ch'ella parli!
Fa' che l'udiamo!
Io l'amo!
Io l'amo!
Io l'amo!

And the ghosts vanish.

THE UNKNOWN PRINCE
(*with a cry*)

No! No! I alone love her! | No! No! Io solo l'amo!

THE MINISTERS
(*prancing around him*)

You love her? What? Who?
Turandot? Ha! Ha! Ha!

L'ami? Che cosa? Chi?
Turandot? Ah! Ah! Ah!

PONG

O insane youth! | O ragazzo demente!

PANG

Turandot doesn't exist! | Turandot non esiste!

PING	
There exists only the Nothingness in which you annihilate yourself . . . !	Non esiste che il Niente, nel quale ti annulli . . . !
PONG AND PANG	
Turandot doesn't exist, doesn't exist!	Turandot non esiste, non esiste!
PING	
Turandot, like all simpletons like yourself! Man! God! I! Peoples! Sovereigns! Pu-Tin-Pao! . . . There exists only the Tao!	Turandot, come tutti quei citrulli tuoi pari! L'uomo! Il Dio! Io! I popoli! I sovrani! Pu-Tin-Pao . . . ! Non esiste che il Tao!
PONG AND PANG	
You annihilate yourself like those simpletons . . .	Tu ti annulli come quei citrulli . . .

THE UNKNOWN PRINCE
(*freeing himself from the Masks*)

For me, the triumph! For me, love!	A me il trionfo! A me l'amore!

He starts to hurl himself toward the gong, but the executioner appears high on the bastion with the severed head of the Prince of Persia.

THE MINISTERS

Fool! There's love! Thus the moon will kiss your face!	Stolto! Ecco l'amore! Così la luna bacerà il tuo volto!

Then Timur, in a desperate impulse, clutching his son, exclaims:

TIMUR

O son, do you then want me, alone, to drag about the world my tortured old age? Help! Is there no human voice that can move your fierce heart?	O figlio, vuoi dunque ch'io solo trascini pel mondo la mia torturata vecchiezza? Aiuto! Non c'è voce umana che muova il tuo cuore feroce?

LIÙ
(*approaching the Prince, imploring, weeping*)

Lord, listen! Ah, Lord, listen! Liù can stand no more! Her heart is breaking! Alas, alas, what a long way with your name in my soul, with your name on my lips! But if your fate is decided tomorrow, we'll die on the road of exile! He will lose his son . . . I, the shadow of a smile! Liù can stand no more! Ah, pity!	Signore, ascolta! Ah, Signore, ascolta! Liù non regge più! Si spezza il cuor! Ahimè, ahimè, quanto cammino col tuo nome nell'anima, col nome tuo sulle labbra! Ma se il tuo destino doman sarà deciso, noi morrem sulla strada dell'esilio! Ei perderà suo figlio . . . io l'ombra d'un sorriso! Liù non regge più! Ah, pietá!

And she bends to the ground, exhausted, sobbing.

THE UNKNOWN PRINCE
(*approaching her, with emotion*)

Don't cry, Liù! If, on one far-off day I smiled at you, for that smile, my sweet girl, listen to me: your Lord	Non piangere, Liù! Se in un lontano giorno io t'ho sorriso, per quel sorriso, dolce mia fanciulla, m'ascolta: Il tuo Signore

will be, tomorrow, perhaps alone in the world . . .
Don't leave him, take him away with you!

sarà, domani, forse solo al mondo . . .
Non lo lasciare, portalo via con te!

LIÙ

We'll die on the road of exile!

Noi morrem sulla strada dell'esilio!

TIMUR

We'll die!

Noi morrem!

THE UNKNOWN PRINCE

Make gentle the roads of exile for him!
This . . this . . oh, my poor Liù,
of your little heart that doesn't fail
he asks who smiles no more . . .
who smiles no more!

Dell'esilio addolcisci a lui le strade!
Questo . . . questo . . . o mia povera Liù,
al tuo piccolo cuore che non cade
chiede colui che non sorride più . . .
che non sorride più!

TIMUR
(*desperately*)

Ah! For the last time!

Ah! per l'ultima volta!

LIÙ

Overcome the horrible spell!

Vinci il fascino orribile!

The ministers, who had moved to one side, now approach the Prince again, praying, insisting.

THE MINISTERS

Life is so beautiful!

La vita è cosi bella!

TIMUR

Have pity on me!

Abbi di me pietà!

LIÙ

Have pity on Liù!

Abbi di Liù pietà!

THE MINISTERS

Life is so beautiful!

La vita è cosi bella!

TIMUR

Have pity on me!
I can't separate myself from you!
I don't want to separate myself from you!
Pity! Pity!
I cast myself moaning at your feet!
Have pity! Don't wish my death!

Abbi di me pietà!
Non posso staccarmi da te!
Non voglio staccarmi da te!
Pietà! Pietà!
Mi getto ai tuoi piedi gemente!
Abbi pietà! non voler la mia morte!

THE UNKNOWN PRINCE

I'm the one who asks for pity!
I no longer listen to anyone!
I see her radiant face!
I see her! She calls me! She's there!
He asks your pardon
who smiles no more!

Son io che domando pietá!
Nessuno più ascolto!
Io vedo il suo fulgido volto!
La vedo! Mi chiama! Essa è là!
Il tuo perdono chiede
colui che non sorride più!

LIÙ

Lord, pity! Have pity on Liù!
Pity on us!

Signore, pietà! Abbi di Liù pietà!
Pietà di noi!

THE MINISTERS

Don't ruin yourself thus!
Seize him! Take him away!
Restrain that raving madman!
Come, take away that madman!
You're mad! Life is so beautiful!

Non perderti cosi!
Afferralo! Portalo via!
Trattieni quel pazzo furente!
Su, porta via quel pazzo!
Folle tu sei! La vita è bella!

The ministers assist the old man and try, with every effort, to drag away the Prince.

PING

Come, a final effort, let's take him away!	Su, un ultimo sforzo, portiamolo via!

THE MINISTERS

Let's take him away!	Portiamolo via!

THE UNKNOWN PRINCE

Let go of me: I've suffered too much! Glory awaits me, awaits me over there!	Lasciatemi: ho troppo sofferto! La gloria m'aspetta, m'aspetta laggiù!

The gong becomes luminous.

TIMUR

You pass over a poor heart that bleeds in vain for you!	Tu passi su un povero cuore che sanguina invano per te!

THE MINISTERS

The face you see is an illusion! The light that gleams is dire!	Il volto che vedi è illusione! La luce che splende è funesta!

THE UNKNOWN PRINCE

There's no human strength that can restrain me! I follow my destiny! I'm all in a fever, I'm all a delirium! Every sense is a fierce torment!	Forza umana non c'è che mi trattenga! Io seguo la mia sorte! Son tutto una febbre, son tutto un delirio! Ogni senso è un martirio feroce!

TIMUR

No one has ever won, no one! On all the sword, the sword swooped down!	Nessuno ha mai vinto, nessuno! Su tutti la spada, la spada piombò!

LIÙ

Ah! Pity! Pity on us! If this torment of his isn't enough, Lord, we are lost! With you!	Ah! Pietà! Pietà di noi! Se questo suo strazio non basta, Signore, noi siamo perduti! Con te!

THE MINISTERS

You risk your destruction, your head! . . . it's a dire illusion! Death, death, death! There is the shadow of the executioner over there!	Tu giochi la tua perdizione, la testa! . . . è illusione funesta! La morte, la morte, la morte! C'è l'ombra del boia laggiù!

THE CROWD
(*within*)

We are already digging the grave for you who want to challenge love! In the darkness is sealed, alas, your cruel fate!	La fossa già scaviam per te che vuoi sfidar l'amor! Nel buio c'è segnato, ahimè, il tuo crudel destin!

LIÙ

Ah let us flee, Lord! Ah! Let us flee!	Ah! fuggiamo, Signore! Ah! fuggiamo!

TIMUR

I cast myself at your feet! Don't wish my death!	Mi getto ai tuoi piedi! Non voler la mia morte!

THE MINISTERS

You are running to your ruin! Don't risk your life!	Tu corri alla rovina! La vita non giocar!

THE UNKNOWN PRINCE

Every fibre of my soul has a voice that cries: Turandot!	Ogni fibra dell'anima ha una voce che grida: Turandot!

ALL

Death! La morte!

THE UNKNOWN PRINCE

Turandot! Turandot!

ALL

Death! La morte!

THE UNKNOWN PRINCE

Turandot! Turandot!

ALL

Death! La morte!

The Prince rushes toward the gong. He seizes the hammer. Like a madman, he strikes three blows. Liù and Timur huddle together in despair. The three ministers, horrified, holding their arms up, flee, exclaiming:

THE MINISTERS

And we'll let him go!	E lasciamolo andar!
Shouting is useless	Inutile è gridar!
in Sanskrit, in Chinese, in the Mongolian language!	in sanscrito, in cinese, in lingua mongola!
When the gong clangs, the executioner rejoices!	Quando rangola il gong la morte gongola!
Ha, ha, ha, ha!	Ah, ah, ah, ah!

THE CROWD
(*within*)

We are already digging the grave for you	La fossa già scaviam per te
who want to challenge love!	che vuoi sfidar l'amor!

The Prince has remained, ecstatic, at the foot of the gong.

Hans Kaart as Calaf at Covent Garden in 1958 (photo: Houston Rogers, Theatre Museum)

Act Two

Scene One. *A pavilion appears, shaped like a vast tent all strangely decorated with symbolic and fantastic Chinese figures. The set is very much downstage and has three openings: one in the centre and one at either side.*

Ping peers in from the centre. And, turning first to the right, then to the left, he calls his companions. They enter, followed by three servants, each carrying a red lantern, a green lantern and a yellow lantern, which they then place symmetrically in the centre of the stage on a low table surrounded by three stools. Then the servants withdraw to the background, where they remain, crouching.

	PING
Hola! Pang! Hola! Pong!	Olà! Pang! Olà! Pong!
	(*and mysteriously*)
Since the dire gong is wakening the palace and wakening the city, let us be ready for every event: if the foreigner wins, for the wedding, and if he loses, for the burial.	Poichè il funesto gong desta la Reggia e desta la città, siam pronti ad ogni evento: se lo straniero vince, per le nozze, e s'egli perde, pel seppellimento.
	PONG (*gaily*)
I'll prepare the wedding!	Io preparo le nozze!
	PANG (*gloomily*)
And I, the obsequies!	Ed io le esequie!
	PONG
The red festival lanterns!	Le rosse lanterne di festa!
	PANG
The white mourning lanterns!	Le bianche lanterne di lutto!
	PONG
The incenses and the offerings ...	Gli incensi e le offerte ...
	PANG
The incenses and the offerings ...	Gli incensi e le offerte ...
	PONG
Paper coins, gilded ...	Monete di carta, dorate ...
	PANG
Tea, sugar, nutmegs!	Thè, zucchero, noci moscate!
	PONG
The handsome scarlet palanquin!	Il bel palanchino scarlatto!
	PANG
The big, well-made bier!	Il feretro, grande, ben fatto!
	PONG
The bonzes who sing ...	I bonzi che cantano ...
	PANG
The bonzes who groan ...	I bonzi che gemono ...
	PONG AND PANG
And all the rest, as the ritual demands ... detailed, infinite!	E tutto quanto il resto, secondo vuole il rito ... minuzioso, infinito!

PING
(*holding his arms up*)

O China, o China, who now leap and start restlessly! How happy you slept, swollen with your seventy-thousand centuries!	O Cina, o Cina, che or sussulti e trasecoli inquieta! Come dormivi lieta, gonfia dei tuoi settantamila secoli!

THE MINISTERS

Everything went according to the very ancient rule of the world . . . then was born . . . then was born . . . then was born Turandot . . . !	Tutto andava secondo L'antichissima regola del mondo . . . Poi naque . . . poi naque . . . poi nacque Turandot . . . !

PING

And for years our holidays are reduced to joys like these:	E sono anni che le nostre feste si riducono a gioie come queste:

PONG

. . . three strokes of the gong . . .	. . . tre battute di gong . . .

PANG

. . . three riddles . . .	. . . tre indovinelli . . .

PING

. . . and off with heads!	. . . e giù teste!

PONG

. . . and off with heads!	. . . e giù teste!

PING

. . . and off with heads!	. . . e giù teste!

All three sit down near the little table on which the servants have set some scrolls. And, as they enumerate, they unroll one or the other volume.

PANG

The Year of the Rat there were six.	L'anno del Topo furon sei.

PONG

The Year of the Dog there were eight!	L'anno del Cane furon otto!

THE MINISTERS

In the current year, the terrible Year of the Tiger, we are already . . .	Nell'anno in corso il terribile anno della Tigre, siamo già . . .

(*counting on their fingers*)

we are already up to the thirteenth, counting the one who is going under! What work! What work! What boredom! What boredom! To what have we been reduced? The ministers of the executioner! Ministers of the executioner!	siamo già al tredicesimo con quello che va sotto! Che lavoro! Che lavoro! Che noia! Che noia! A che siamo ridotti? I ministri del boia? Ministri del boia!

They drop the scrolls and sink down, comically nostalgic.

PING
(*absorbed in a distant vision*)

I have a house in Honan with its little blue lake all girdled with bamboo . . . And I am here wasting my life, racking my brain over the sacred books . . .	Ho una casa nell'Honan con il suo laghetto blu tutto cinto di bambù . . . E sto qui a dissipar la mia vita, a stillarmi il cervel sui libri sacri . . .

	PANG AND PONG	
. . . over the sacred books . . .		. . . sui libri sacri . . .
	PING	
. . . over the sacred books . . . And I could go back down there . . .		. . . sui libri sacri . . . E potrei tornar laggiù . . .
	PANG AND PONG	
Go back down there!		Tornar laggiù!
	PING	
. . . to my little blue lake . . .		. . . presso il mio laghetto blu . . .
	PANG AND PONG	
Go back down there!		Tornar laggiù!
	PING	
. . . all girdled with bamboo!		. . . tutto cinto di bambù!
	PONG	
I have forests, near Tsiang, than which none is more beautiful, which have no shade for me.		Ho foreste, presso Tsiang, che più belle non ce n'è! che non hanno ombra per me.
	PANG	
I have a garden near Kiù which I left to come here and which I'll never see again!		Ho un giardino presso Kiù che lasciai per venir qui e che non rivedrò mai più!
	PING	
. . . and I could go back down there to my little blue lake! All girdled with bamboo!		. . . e potrei tornar laggiù presso il mio laghetto blu! Tutto cinto di bambù!
	THE MINISTERS	
And we are here . . . racking our brains over the sacred books!		E stiam qui . . . a stillarci il cervel sui libri sacri!
	PONG	
And I could go back to Tsiang . . .		E potrei tornare a Tsiang . . .
	PING	
And I could go back down there . . .		E potrei tornar laggiù . . .
	PANG	
And I could go back to Kiù . . .		E potrei tornar a Kiù . . .
	PING	
. . . to enjoy my blue lake . . .		. . . a godermi il lago blu . . .
	PONG	
Tsiang . . .		Tsiang . . .
	PANG	
Kiù . . .		Kiù . . .
	PING	
Honan . . . all girdled with bamboo!		Honan . . . tutto cinto di bambù!
	PONG	
And I could go back to Tsiang!		E potrei tornare a Tsiang!
	PANG	
And I could go back to Kiù!		E potrei tornare a Kiù!

They rise and with a broad, disconsolate gesture, exclaim:

THE MINISTERS

O world full of mad lovers!	O mondo pieno di pazzi innamorati!

PONG AND PANG

We have . . . seen plenty of suitors arrive!	Ne abbiam . . . visti arrivar degli aspiranti!

PING

Oh, how many!	O quanti!

PONG

Oh, how many!	O quanti!

PING

We have seen plenty of suitors arrive!	Ne abbiam visti arrivar degli aspiranti!

PANG

Oh, how many, oh, how many!	O quanti, o quanti!

PONG

Oh, how many!	O quanti!

PING

O world full of mad lovers! Do you remember the royal Prince of Samarkand? He made his request! And she, with what joy, sent him to the executioner!	O mondo pieno di pazzi innamorati! Vi ricordate il principe regal di Samarcanda? Fece la sua domanda! E lei, con quale gioia, gli mandò il boia!

VOICES WITHIN

Oil, sharpen, let the blade flash, spurt fire and blood!	Ungi, arrota, che la lama guizzi, sprizzi fuoco e sangue!

PONG

And the bejewelled Indian Sagarika, with earrings like little bells? He asked for love, he was decapitated!	E l'indiano gemmato Sagarika, cogli orecchini come campanelli? Amore chiese, fu decapitato!

PANG

And the Burmese?	Ed il birmano?

PONG

And the Prince of the Kirghiz?	E il prence dei Kirghisi?

PONG AND PANG

Killed! Killed! Killed! Killed!	Uccisi! Uccisi! Uccisi! Uccisi!

PING

And the Tartar with the six-cubit bow, girdled with rich hides?	E il tartaro dall'arco di sei cubiti, di ricche pelli cinto?

VOICES WITHIN

Where reigns Turandot work never languishes!	Dove regna Turandot, il lavoro mai non langue!

PONG

Executed!	Estinto!

PANG

Executed!	Estinto!

PING

And decapitate ...	E decapita ...

PANG

Kill and execute ...	Uccidi e estingui ...

PONG

Slaughter ... slaughter!	Ammazza ... ammazza!

PING

Kill! Slaughter!	Uccidi! Ammazza!

THE MINISTERS

Farewell, love ... ! Farewell, race! Farewell, divine race! And China ends!	Addio, amore ... ! addio, razza! Addio, stirpe divina! E finisce la Cina!

They sit down again. Only Ping remains standing, as if to give more value to his invocation.

PING
(*holding his arms up*)

O Tigress! O Tigress!	O Tigre! O Tigre!

PONG AND PANG

O great She-Marshal of Heaven! Grant that it arrive, the great, awaited night, the night of surrender ...	O grande Marescialla del Cielo! Fa' che giunga la gran notte attesa, la notte della resa ...

PING

I want to prepare the nuptial bed for her!	Il talamo le voglio preparare!

PONG
(*with an obvious gesture*)

I'll plump up the soft feathers for her!	Sprimaccerò per lei le molli piume!

PANG
(*as if scattering perfumes*)

I want to perfume her bedchamber!	Io l'alcova le voglio profumare!

PING

I'll lead the bridal pair, carrying the light!	Gli sposi guiderò reggendo il lume!

THE MINISTERS

Then, all three, in the garden, we'll sing ...	Poi tutt'e tre, in giardino, noi canterem ...

PONG

... we'll sing of love till morning ...	... canteremo d'amor fino al mattino ...

PING

Like this ...	Cosi ...

PANG

Like this ...	Cosi ...

Ping stands on the stool, the other two seated at his feet.

THE MINISTERS

No longer in China, to our good luck, is there a women who rejects love! There was only one and this one who was ice now is flame and ardour!	Non v'è in Cina, per nostra fortuna, donna più che rinneghi l'amor! Una sola ce n'era e quest'una che fu ghiaccio, ora è vampa ed ardor!
Princess, your empire stretches from the Tse-Kiang to the immense Yangtze!	Principessa, il tuo impero si stende dal Tse-Kiang all'immenso Jang-Tse!

PING

But there, within the soft draperies, there is a husband who rules over you!	Ma là, dentro alle soffici tende, c'è uno sposo che impera su te!

THE MINISTERS

You already smell the aroma of kisses, already you are tamed, you are all languor!	Tu dei baci già senti l'aroma, già sei doma, sei tutto languor!

PONG AND PANG

Glory to the secret night which now sees the wonder accomplished!	Gloria alla notte segreta che il prodigio ora vede compir!

PING AND PANG

Glory to the secret night!	Gloria alla notte segreta!

PONG

To the yellow coverlet of silk, witness to the sweet sighs!	Alla gialla coperta di seta testimone dei dolci sospir!

THE MINISTERS

Everything whispers in the garden and golden campanulas tinkle . . . They whisper amorous words to one another . . .	Nel giardin sussurran le cose e tintinnan campanule d'or . . . Si sospiran parole amorose . . .

PING

. . . the flowers are beaded with dew!	. . . di rugiada s'imperlano i fiori!

THE MINISTERS

Glory to the beautiful, unclad body which now knows the mystery it was ignorant of! Glory to the ecstasy and to love which has won, and restores peace to China . . .	Gloria al bel corpo discinto che il mistero ignorato ora sa! Gloria all'ebbrezza e all'amore che ha vinto, e alla Cina la pace ridà . . .

But from within the sound of the palace reawakening recalls the three Ministers to the sad reality. And then Ping, leaping to the ground, exclaims:

PING

We're dreaming! And the palace already teems with lanterns, with servants and with soldiers! Hear: the great drum of the Green Temple! Already the infinite slippers of Peking are clattering!	Noi si sogna! E il Palazzo già formicola di lanterne, di servi e di soldati! Udite: il gran tamburo del Tempio Verde! Già stridon le infinite ciabatte di Pekino!

PONG

Hear the trumpets! Peace, indeed!	Udite le trombe! Altro che pace!

PANG

The ceremony is beginning!	Ha inizio la ceremonia!

THE MINISTERS

Let us go to enjoy the umpteenth torture!	Andiamo a goderci l'ennesimo supplizio!

They go off, without enthusiasm.

Scene Two. *The vast square of the royal palace appears. Almost in the centre there is a huge marble stairway, which is lost at its summit among triple arches. The stairway has three broad landings. Numerous servants set varicoloured lanterns on all sides. The crowd, little by little,* *invades the square. The mandarins arrive, in their blue and gold garments. At the top of the steps, very tall and pompous, the Eight Sages appear. They are old, almost exactly alike, enormous and massive. Their gestures are very slow and simultaneous. Each has three silk scrolls, sealed, in his hand. These are the scrolls that contain the solution to Turandot's riddles.*

THE CROWD
(*commenting on the arrival of the various dignitaries*)

Grave, enormous and imposing with the mystery of the sealed riddles already the Sages advance . . .	Gravi, enormi ed imponenti col mister dei chiusi enigmi già s'avanzano i Sapienti . . .

Incense begins to rise from the tripods that are set at the top of the stairs. Amid the clouds of incense the three ministers make their way, now wearing their yellow ceremonial dress.

THE CROWD

There's Ping! There's Pong! There's Pang!	Ecco Ping! Ecco Pong! Ecco Pang!

Amid the clouds of perfume the yellow and white standards of the Emperor are seen arriving. Slowly the incense clears away and then, at the top of the steps, appears, seated on a broad ivory throne, Emperor Altoum. He is very old, all white, venerable, hieratic. He seems a god who appears from among the clouds.

THE CROWD

Ten thousand years to our Emperor!	Diecimila anni al nostro Imperatore!

The whole crowd prostrates itself on the ground in an attitude of great respect.

Glory to you!	Gloria a te!

The square is suffused by a warm light. The Unknown Prince is at the foot of the steps. Timur and Liù, at left, mix with the crowd.

THE EMPEROR
(*slow, in a faint and distant voice*)

An atrocious oath forces me to keep faith with the grim pact. And the holy sceptre that I clasp streams with blood! Enough of blood! Young man, go!	Un giuramento atroce mi costringe a tener fede al fosco patto. E il santo scettro ch'io stringo, gronda di sangue! Basta sangue! Giovine, va'!

THE UNKNOWN PRINCE
(*firmly*)

Son of Heaven, I ask to face the trial!	Figlio del Cielo, io chiedo d'affrontar la prova!

THE EMPEROR
(*almost imploring*)

Allow me to die without bearing the weight of your young life!	Fa' ch'io possa morir senza portare il peso della tua giovine vita!

THE UNKNOWN PRINCE
(*more strongly*)

Son of Heaven! I ask to face the trial!	Figlio del Cielo! Io chiedo d'affrontar la prova!

THE EMPEROR

Don't wish that again the palace, the world be filled with horror!	Non voler che s'empia ancor d'orror la Reggia, il mondo!

THE UNKNOWN PRINCE
(*with mounting strength*)

Son of Heaven! I ask to face the trial!	Figlio del Cielo! Io chiedo d'affrontar la prova!

THE EMPEROR
(*with wrath, but with grandeur*)

Foreigner, drunk with death! So be it! Let your destiny
be fulfilled!

Straniero ebbro di morte! E sia! Si compia
il tuo destino!

THE CROWD

Ten thousand years to our Emperor!

Diecimila anni al nostro Imperatore!

A procession of women dressed in white appears from the palace and spreads out along the stairs: they are Turandot's handmaidens. Amid the general silence the mandarin advances.

THE MANDARIN

People of Peking!
This is the law: Turandot, the Pure,
will be the bride of the man, of royal blood,
who solves the three riddles that she will propose.
But he who faces the trial and remains defeated,
must offer his haughty head to the axe!

Popolo di Pekino!
Le legge è questa: Turandot, la Pura,
sposa sarà di chi, di sangue regio,
spieghi gli enigmi ch'ella proporrà.
Ma chi affronta il cimento e vinto resta,
porga alla scure la superba testa!

BOYS
(*within*)

From the desert to the sea
don't you hear a thousand voices sigh:
'Princess, come down to me!
Everything will shine!'

Dal deserto al mar
non odi mille voci sospirar:
'Principessa, scendi a me!
Tutto splenderà!'

Turandot advances and places herself before the throne. Very beautiful, impassive, she looks with very cold eyes at the Prince, who, dazzled at first, gradually regains his self-control and stares at her with ardent determination. Timur and Liù cannot take their eyes, their very souls, from the Prince. In the solemn silence Turandot says:

TURANDOT

In this palace, a thousand, thousand years ago,
a desperate cry resounded.
And that cry, through descendant and descendant,
took refuge here in my soul!

In questa Reggia, or son mill'anni e mille,
un grido disperato risonò.
E quel grido, traverso stirpe e stirpe,
qui nell'anima mia si rifugiò!

Princess Lo-u-Ling,
sweet and serene ancestress, who reigned
in your dark silence, in pure joy,
and who defied, inflexible and sure,
bitter domination, you relive in me today!

Principessa Lo-u-Ling,
ava dolce e serena, che regnavi
nel tuo cupo silenzio, in gioia pura,
e sfidasti inflessibile e sicura
l'aspro dominio, oggi rivivi in me!

THE CROWD
(*softly*)

It was when the King of the Tartars
unfurled his seven flags!

Fu quando il Re dei Tartari
le sette sue bandiere dispiegò!

TURANDOT
(*like something remote*)

Still, in the time that everyone remembers,
there was alarm and terror and the rumble of arms!
The kingdom defeated! The kingdom defeated!
And Lo-u-Ling, my ancestress, dragged away
by a man like you, like you, foreigner,
there in the atrocious night,
where her fresh voice was extinguished!

Pure, nel tempo che ciascun ricorda,
fu sgomento e terrore e rombo d'armi!
Il Regno vinto! Il Regno vinto!
E Lo-u-Ling, la mia ava, trascinata
da un uomo come te, come te, straniero,
là nella notte atroce,
dove si spense la sua fresca voce!

THE CROWD
(murmurs reverently)

For centuries she has slept in her enormous tomb!	Da secoli Ella dorme nella sua tomba enorme!

TURANDOT

O Princes who in long caravans from every part of the world come here to try your fate, I avenge upon you, upon you that purity, that cry and that death!	O Principi che a lunghe carovane d'ogni parte del mondo qui venite a gettar la vostra sorte, io vendico su voi, su voi quella purezza, quel grido e quella morte!
No one will ever possess me! The horror of him who killed her is alive in my heart! No, no! No one will ever possess me!	Mai nessun m'avrà! L'orror di chi l'uccise vivo nel cor mi sta! No, no! Mai nessun m'avrà!
Ah, in me is reborn the pride of such purity!	Ah, rinasce in me l'orgoglio di tanta purità!

(and, threateningly, to the Prince:)

Stranger! Don't tempt fate! 'The riddles are three, death is one!'	Straniero! Non tentar la fortuna! 'Gli enigmi sono tre, la morte è una!'

THE UNKNOWN PRINCE

No! no! The riddles are three, one is life!	No! no! Gli enigmi sono tre, una è la vita!

TURANDOT

No! No! The riddles are three, death is one!	No! No! Gli enigmi sono tre, la morte è una!

THE UNKNOWN PRINCE

The riddles are three, one is life!	Gli enigmi sono tre, una è la vita!

THE CROWD

Offer the bold trial to the foreign prince, O Turandot! Turandot!	Al Principe straniero offri la prova ardita, O Turandot! Turandot!

The trumpets blare. Silence. Turandot proclaims the first riddle.

TURANDOT

Stranger, listen! 'In the gloomy night an iridescent ghost flies. It rises and spreads its wings over the black, infinite mankind. All the world invokes it, and all the world implores it! But the ghost vanishes with the dawn to be reborn in the heart! And every night it is born and every day it dies . . .'	Straniero, ascolta! 'Nella cupa notte vola un fantasma iridiscente. Sale e dispiega l'ale sulla nera, infinita umanità. Tutto il mondo l'invoca e tutto il mondo l'implora! Ma il fantasma sparisce coll'aurora per rinascere nel cuore! Ed ogni notte nasce ed ogni giorno muore . . .'

THE UNKNOWN PRINCE
(with sudden confidence)

Yes! It is reborn! It is reborn! And in triumph it carries me away with itself, Turandot, 'Hope.'	Sì! Rinasce! Rinasce! E in esultanza mi porta via con sè, Turandot, 'La Speranza.'

THE SAGES
(stand up and rhythmically open together the first scroll)

Hope! Hope! Hope!	La speranza! La speranza! La speranza!

Then, together, they sit down again. A murmur runs through the crowd, repressed promptly by a dignitary's gesture.

TURANDOT
(*turns her eyes full of pride. She laughs a cold laugh. Her haughty superiority grips her again.*)

Yes! Hope, which always disappoints!	Si! La speranza che delude sempre!

(*And then, as if to bewitch and daze the Prince, she nervously comes half-way down the stairs. And there she asks the second riddle:*)

'It darts like a flame, and is not a flame! At times it is delirium! It's a fever of impulse and ardour! Inertia transforms it into languor! If you are lost or die, it grows cold! If you dream of conquest, it flames! It has a voice that you listen to in fear and the vivid glow of the sunset . . .'	'Guizza al pari di fiamma, e non è fiamma! È talvolta delirio! È febbre d'impeto e ardore! L'inerzia lo tramuta in un languore! Se ti perdi o trapassi, si raffredda! Se sogni la conquista avvampa, Ha una voce che trepido tu ascolti, e del tramonto il vivido baglior . . .'

The Prince hesitates. Turandot's gaze seems to confound him. He seeks. He doesn't find. The Princess assumes an expression of triumph.

THE EMPEROR

Don't destroy yourself, foreigner!	Non perderti, straniero!

THE CROWD

It's for your life! It's for your life! Speak! Don't destroy yourself, foreigner! Speak! Speak!	È per la vita! È per la vita! Parla! Non perderti, straniero! Parla! Parla!

LIÙ

It's for love!	È per l'amore!

THE UNKNOWN PRINCE
(*He suddenly loses his agonised, lost expression. And he cries to Turandot:*)

Yes, Princess! It flames and also languishes, in my veins, if you look at me. 'Blood!'	Si, Principessa! Avvampa e insieme langue, se tu mi guardi, nelle vene! 'Il Sangue.'

THE SAGES
(*opening the second scroll*)

Blood! Blood! Blood!	Il sangue! Il sangue! Il sangue!

THE CROWD
(*bursting out, joyously*)

Courage, solver of riddles!	Coraggio, scioglitore degli enigmi!

TURANDOT
(*stiffening, as if struck by a lash, shouts to the guards:*)

Strike those wretches!	Percuotete quei vili!

And saying this, she runs down the steps. The Prince falls to his knees. And she bends over him, and fiercely, hammering out the syllables, her mouth almost on his face, she asks the third riddle.

TURANDOT

'Frost that sets you afire! And from your fire gains more than frost! White and dark! If it wants you free, it makes you more enslaved! If it accepts you for slave, it makes you king!'	'Gelo che ti dà foco! E dal tuo foco più gelo prende! Candida ed oscura! Se libero ti vuol, ti fa più servo! Se per servo t'accetta, ti fa Re!'

The Unknown Prince is no longer breathing. He no longer answers. Turandot is upon him, bent as if over her prey.

The 'Riddle' scene in Act Two at La Scala, 1983, with Ghena Dimitrova as Turandot (Archivio Fotografico Teatro alla Scala)

Gianna Arangi-Lombardi as Turandot and Francesco Merli as Calaf in Australia in 1928 (Stuart-Liff Collection)

TURANDOT
(*sneering*)

Come, foreigner! Fear makes you blanch!
And you feel yourself lost! Come, foreigner,
the frost that gives fire — what is it?

Su, straniero! Ti sbianca la paura!
E ti senti perduto! Su, straniero,
il gelo che dà foco, che cos'è?

THE UNKNOWN PRINCE
(*Desolate, he has bowed his head in his hands. But it is only for a moment. A flash of joy illuminates him. He springs to his feet, magnificent in pride and strength. He exclaims:*)

My victory now has given you to me!
My fire thaws you:
'Turandot!'

La mia vittoria ormai t'ha data a me!
Il mio fuoco ti sgela:
'Turandot!'

Turandot staggers, steps back, remains motionless at the foot of the steps, numb with contempt and grief.

THE SAGES
(*who have unrolled the third scroll, exclaim:*)

Turandot!
Turandot!
Turandot!

Turandot!
Turandot!
Turandot!

THE CROWD

Turandot! Turandot!
Glory, glory, O victor!
May life smile upon you!
May love smile upon you!
Ten thousand years to our Emperor!
Light, King of all the world!

Turandot! Turandot!
Gloria, gloria, O vincitore!
Ti sorrida la vita!
Ti sorrida l'amor!
Diecimila anni al nostro Imperatore!
Luce, Re di tutto il mondo!

TURANDOT
(*has stirred at the first cry. Breathlessly she climbs the steps. She is near the Emperor's throne. She cries out:*)

Son of Heaven! August Father! No!
Don't cast your daughter into the arms
of the foreigner!

Figlio del Cielo! Padre augusto! No!
Non gettar tua figlia nelle braccia
dello straniero!

THE EMPEROR
(*solemnly*)

The oath is sacred!

È sacro il giuramento!

TURANDOT
(*with vehemence, with rebellion*)

No! Don't say so! Your daughter is sacred!
You can't give me to him like a slave girl,
dying of shame!

No! Non dire! Tua figlia è sacra!
Non puoi donarmi a lui come una schiava
morente di vergogna!

(*to the Prince*)

Don't look at me like that!
You who mock my pride!
I won't be yours!
No! I don't want to!

Non guardarmi cosi!
Tu che irridi al mio orgoglio!
Non sarò tua!
No! Non voglio!

THE EMPEROR
(*rising to his feet*)

The oath is sacred!

È sacro il giuramento!

THE CROWD

The oath is sacred!

È sacro il giuramento!

TURANDOT

No, don't look at me like that, I won't be yours!

No, non guardarmi cosi, non sarò tua!

THE CROWD

He's won, Princess!
He offered his life for you!

Ha vinto, Principesa!
Offri per te la vita!

TURANDOT

No one will ever possess me! | Mai nessun m'avrà!

THE CROWD

Be the reward of his daring!
He offered his life for you!
The oath is sacred!

Sia premio al suo ardimento!
Offrì per te la vita!
È sacro il giuramento!

TURANDOT
(*again addressing the Prince*)

Do you want me in your arms by force,
reluctant, shuddering?

Mi vuoi nelle tue braccia a forza
riluttante, fremente?

THE UNKNOWN PRINCE
(*with bold impetuousness*)

No, no, haughty princess!
I want you all ardent
with love!

No, no, Principessa altera!
Ti voglio tutta ardente
d'amor!

THE CROWD

Brave one!
Bold!
Brave!
Oh, strong one!

Coraggioso!
Audace!
Coraggioso!
O forte!

THE UNKNOWN PRINCE

You asked me three riddles, and three I solved!
I'll ask you only one:
you don't know my name! Tell me my name,
before the dawn! And, at dawn, I'll die!

Tre enigmi m'hai proposto! e tre ne sciolsi!
Uno soltanto a te ne proporrò:
il mio nome non sai! Dimmi il mio nome,
prima dell'alba! E all'alba morirò!

Amid intense expectancy Turandot bows her head, assenting. Then, the old Emperor rises and, with heartbroken emotion, says:

THE EMPEROR

May Heaven will that, at the first sunlight,
you be my son!

Il cielo voglia che col primo sole
mio figlio tu sia!

The court rises. The trumpets blow. The flags sway. The Prince, his head high, with firm step, climbs the staircase, while the imperial anthem bursts forth, solemn, sung by the whole populace.

THE CROWD

At your feet we prostrate ourselves,
Light, King of all the world!
For your wisdom,
for your goodness,
we give ourselves to you,
happy, in humility!

Ai tuoi piedi ci prostriam,
Luce, Re di tutto il mondo!
Per la tua saggezza,
per la tua bontà,
ci doniamo a te,
lieti, in umiltà!

Let our love rise to you!
Ten thousand years to our Emperor!

A te salga il nostro amor!
Diecimila anni al nostro Imperatore!

To you, heir of Hien Wang,
we cry:
Ten thousand years to the great Emperor!
High, high the flags!
Glory to you! Glory to you!

A te, erede di Hien Wang,
noi gridiam:
Diecimila anni al grande Imperatore!
Alte, alte le bandiere!
Gloria a te! Gloria a te!

Act Three

Scene One. *The garden of the royal palace, very vast, all rolling slopes, bushes and the dark outlines of bronze divinities, faintly illuminated from below by the reflection from the incense braziers. At right rises a pavilion which is reached by five steps and bounded by a richly embroidered hanging. The pavilion is the forepart of one of the buildings of the palace, on the side toward the rooms of Turandot.*

It is night. From the farthest distances come voices of heralds who are going through the immense city issuing the royal command. Other voices, near and far, echo these.

Lying on the steps of the pavilion is the Prince. In the great nocturnal silence he listens to the cries of the heralds, as if he were almost no longer living in reality.

THE VOICES OF THE HERALDS

Thus commands Turandot:
'This night let no one sleep in Peking!'

Cosi comanda Turandot:
'Questa notte nessun dorma in Pekino!'

DISTANT VOICES
(*like a lament*)

Let no one sleep!
Let no one sleep!

Nessun dorma!
Nessun dorma!

THE VOICES OF THE HERALDS

'Under pain of death, the stranger's name
must be revealed before morning!'

'Pena la morte, il nome dell'Ignoto
sia rivelato prima del mattino!'

DISTANT VOICES

Under pain of death!
Under pain of death!

Pena la morte!
Pena la morte!

THE VOICES OF THE HERALDS

'This night let no one sleep in Peking!'

'Questa notte nessun dorma in Pekino!'

DISTANT VOICES

Let no one sleep!
Let no one sleep!

Nessun dorma!
Nessun dorma!

THE UNKNOWN PRINCE

Let no one sleep! . . . You too, O Princess,
in your cold room
are looking at the stars
that tremble with love and with hope!

But my mystery is locked in me,
no one will know my name!
No, no, upon your mouth I'll say it
when the light shines!
And my kiss will break the silence
that makes you mine! . . .

Nessun dorma! . . . Tu pure, O Principessa,
nella tua fredda stanza
guardi le stelle
che tremano d'amore e di speranza!

Ma il mio mistero è chiuso in me,
il nome mio nessun saprà!
No, no, sulla tua bocca lo dirò
quando la luce splenderà!
Ed il mio bacio scioglierà il silenzio
che ti fa mia . . . !

WOMEN'S VOICES
(*mysterious and remote*)

No one will know his name . . .
And we, alas, shall have to die, to die . . . !

Il nome suo nessun saprà . . .
E noi dovrem, ahimè, morir, morir . . . !

THE UNKNOWN PRINCE

Dissolve, O Night . . . !
Set, stars!
At dawn I'll win!

Dilegua, O notte . . . !
Tramontate, stelle!
All'alba vincerò!

Gliding among the bushes, some shadows appear, confused forms in the darkness of the night, which become more and more numerous and finally turn into a crowd. The three ministers are at its head.

PING
(*sidles up to the prince*)

You who look at the stars,
lower your eyes!

Tu che guardi le stelle,
abbassa gli occhi!

PONG

Our life is in your power!

La nostra vita è in tuo potere!

PANG

Our life!

La nostra vita!

PING

Did you hear the proclamation?
Through Peking's streets death raps
at every door and cries: the name!

Udiste il bando?
Per le vie di Pekino ad ogni porta
batte la morte e grida: il nome!

THE MINISTERS

The name, or blood!

Il nome o sangue!

THE UNKNOWN PRINCE

What do you want of me?

Che volete da me?

PING

You say what you want!

Di' tu, che vuoi!

PONG

You say what you want!

Di' tu che vuoi!

PING

Is it love you seek?

È l'amore che cerchi?

PANG

You say: what do you want?

Di' tu, che vuoi?

PING

You say: what do you want?
Very well: take!

Di' tu, che vuoi?
Ebbene: prendi!

And he thrusts a group of very beautiful, half-naked, provocative maidens at the Prince's feet.

PING

Look . . . ! They are beautiful!
They are beautiful amid shining veils!

Guarda . . . ! son belle!
Son belle fra lucenti veli!

PONG AND PANG

Supple bodies!

Corpi flessuosi!

PING

All ecstasies and promises
of wondrous embraces!

Tutte ebbrezze e promesse
d'amplessi prodigiosi!

THE MAIDENS
(*surrounding the Prince*)

Ah, ah! Ah, ah!

Ah, ah! Ah, ah!

THE UNKNOWN PRINCE
(*with a movement of rebellion*)

No . . . ! No . . . !

No . . . ! No . . . !

PONG AND PANG

What do you want?

Che vuoi?

THE MINISTERS

Riches?
All treasures for you!

Ricchezze?
Tutti i tesori a te!

At a sign from Ping sacks, coffers, baskets brimming with gold and gems are carried before the Prince. And the three ministers make these splendours flash before his dazzled eyes.

PING

They break the black night . . .	Rompon la notte nera . . .

PONG

Blue fires!	Fuochi azzurri!

PING

. . . these bright gems!	. . . queste fulgide gemme!

PANG

Green splendours!	Verdi splendori!

PONG

Pale hyacinths!	Pallidi giacinti!

PANG

The rubies' red flames!	Le vampe rosse dei rubini!

PING

They are stars' drops!	Sono gocciole d'astri!

PONG AND PANG

Blue fires!	Fuochi azzurri!

PING

Take! It's all yours!	Prendi! È tutto tuo!

THE UNKNOWN PRINCE
(*rebelling again*)

No! No riches! No!	No! nessuna ricchezza! No!

THE MINISTERS

Do you want glory? We'll have you escape!	Vuoi la gloria? Noi ti farem fuggir!

PONG AND PANG

And you'll go far off with the stars toward fabulous empires!	E andrai lontano con le stelle verso imperi favolosi!

THE CROWD

Flee! Flee! Go far off! And all of us will be saved!	Fuggi! Fuggi! Va' lontano! e noi tutti ci salviam!

THE UNKNOWN PRINCE
(*holding his arms up to heaven*)

Dawn, come! Dissolve this nightmare . . . !	Alba, vieni! Quest'incubo dissolvi . . . !

Then the three ministers huddle around him with mounting, threatening despair.

PING

Foreigner, you don't know, what the Cruel One is capable of, you don't know . . .	Straniero, tu non sai, di che cosa è capace la Crudele, tu non sai . . .

PONG AND PANG

You don't know what horrible tortures China may invent if you remain and don't reveal your name to us!	Tu non sai quali orrendi martiri la Cina inventi se tu rimani e non ci sveli il nome!

THE MINISTERS, CROWD

The Sleepless One doesn't forgive! We're lost! It will be horrible torture! The sharp irons! The bristling wheels!	L'Insonne non perdona! Siam perduti! Sarà martirio orrendo! I ferri aguzzi! L'irte ruote!

The hot grip of the pincers!	Il caldo morso delle tenaglie!
Death in little sips!	La morte a sorso a sorso!
Don't make us die!	Non farci morire!

THE UNKNOWN PRINCE
(*with supreme firmness*)

Useless prayers!	Inutili preghiere!
Useless threats!	Inutili minacce!
Should the world collapse, I want Turandot!	Crollasse il mondo, voglio Turandot!

Then the crowd loses all restraint, and it yells savagely, surrounding the Prince:

THE CROWD

You won't have her!	Non l'avrai!
No, you won't have her!	No, non l'avrai!
You'll die before us! You, accursed!	Morrai prima di noi! Tu maledetto!
You'll die before us, you, pitiless!	Morrai prima di noi, tu spietato!
Cruel!	Crudele!
The name!	Il nome!
Speak!	Parla!
The name!	Il nome!

High and menacing, daggers are stretched out toward the Prince, enclosed in the fierce and desperate circle. But suddenly tumultuous cries are heard from the garden, and all stop.

THE GUARDS

Here's the name! It's here! It's here!	Eccolo il nome! È qua! È qua!

A group of hired assassins drag in old Timur and Liù, worn, beaten, exhausted, bloodstained. The crowd falls silent in the anxiety of waiting. The Prince rushes over, shouting:

THE UNKNOWN PRINCE

They don't know . . . ! They don't know my name!	Costor non sanno . . . ! Ignorano il mio nome!

But Ping, who recognizes the two, drunk with joy, replies:

PING

They are the old man and the young girl	Sono il vecchio e la giovane
who were talking with you yesterday evening!	che iersera parlavano con te!

THE UNKNOWN PRINCE

Let them go!	Lasciateli!

PING

They know the secret!	Conoscono il segreto!
(*to the guards*)	
Where did you catch them?	Dove li avete colti?

THE GUARDS

While they wandered there, near the walls!	Mentre erravano là, presso le mura!

THE MINISTERS
(*running to the pavilion*)

Princess!	Principessa!

THE MINISTERS, CROWD

Princess!	Principessa!

Turandot appears at the edge of the pavilion. All prostrate themselves on the ground. Only Ping, advancing with extreme humility, says:

PING

Divine Princess! The stranger's name	Principessa divina! Il nome dell'ignoto
is closed in these silent mouths.	sta chiuso in queste bocche silenti.
And we have irons to wrench out those teeth,	E abbiamo ferri per schiodar quei denti,
and we have hooks to tear out that name!	e uncini abbiamo per strappar quel nome!

The Prince, who had controlled himself so as not to give himself away, now, at hearing this cruel contempt and menace, makes a movement of impetuous rebellion. But Turandot stops him with a look of imperiousness and irony.

TURANDOT

You're pale, foreigner!	Sei pallido, straniero!

THE UNKNOWN PRINCE
(*haughtily*)

Your alarm sees dawn's pallor on my face! They don't know me!	Il tuo sgomento vede il pallor dell'alba sul mio volto! Costor non mi conoscono!

TURANDOT

We'll see!	Vedremo!

(*and, addressing Timur, with very firm command*)

Come! Speak, old man!	Su! Parla, vecchio!

She waits, sure, almost indifferent. But the old man is silent. Dazed with grief, pale, dirty, bruised, his venerable white hair dishevelled, he looks mutely at the Princess, his eyes wise with an expression of desperate supplication.

TURANDOT
(*with fury, to the ministers*)

I want him to speak! The name!	Io voglio ch'egli parli! Il nome!

Timur is seized again but, before the Prince has time to move to hurl himself forward and defend him, Liù advances rapidly toward Turandot.

LIÙ

The name that you seek only I know.	Il nome che cercate io sola so.

THE CROWD

Our life is saved! The nightmare's vanished!	La vita è salva! L'incubo svanì!

THE UNKNOWN PRINCE
(*with haughty reproof, to Liù*)

You know nothing, slave!	Tu non sai nulla, schiava!

LIÙ
(*looks at the Prince with infinite tenderness, then, turning to Turandot*)

I know his name . . . It is a supreme delight for me to keep it a secret and to possess it, alone!	Io so il suo nome . . . M'è suprema delizia tenerlo segreto e possederlo io sola!

THE CROWD
(*which sees its hope vanishing, bursts towards Liù, shouting*)

Let her be bound! Let her be tortured! That she may speak! That she may die!	Sia legata! Sia straziata! Perchè parli! Perchè muoia!

THE UNKNOWN PRINCE
(*placing himself before Liù*)

You'll pay for her tears! You'll pay for her torments!	Sconterete le sue lagrime! Sconterete i suoi tormenti!

TURANDOT
(*violent, to the guards*)

Hold him!	Tenetelo!

The Prince is seized by the guards and held fast, bound. Then Turandot resumes her hieratic almost absent, attitude, as Liù, gripped by her torturers, has sunk to the ground on her knees.

LIÙ
(firmly, to the Prince)

Lord, I won't speak!	Signor, non parlerò!

PING
(bent over her)

That name!	Quel nome!

LIÙ

No!	No!

PING

That name!	Quel nome!

LIÙ

Your servant asks forgiveness, but she cannot obey!	La tua serva chiede perdono, ma obbedir non può!

At a sign from Ping, the assassins seize her, twist her arms. Liù screams.

TIMUR
(stirs from his terrible silence)

Why are you crying?	Perchè gridi?

THE UNKNOWN PRINCE

Let her go!	Lasciatela!

LIÙ

No . . . no . . . I won't cry any more! They aren't hurting me! No, no one is touching me . . .	No . . . no . . . Non grido più! Non mi fan male No, nessun mi tocca . . .

(to the guards)

Twist harder . . . but close my mouth so that he won't hear me!	Stringete . . . ma chiudetemi la bocca ch'ei non mi senta!

(then, exhausted)

I can stand no more!	Non resisto più!

THE CROWD

Speak! His name!	Parla! Il suo nome!

TURANDOT

Free her! Speak!	Sia lasciata! Parla!

LIÙ

I'd rather die!	Piuttosto morrò!

And she sinks down near the steps of the pavilion.

TURANDOT
(staring at Liù, as if to gaze into her mystery)

Who placed such strength in your heart?	Chi pose tanta forza nel tuo cuore?

LIÙ

Princess — love!	Principessa, l'amore!

TURANDOT

Love?	L'amore?

LIÙ
(raising her eyes, filled with tenderness)

Such love — secret and unconfessed, so great that these tortures are sweetnesses for me, because I present them to my Lord . . . Because, remaining silent, I give him your love . . . I give him you, Princess, and I lose all,	Tanto amore segreto, e inconfessato, grande cosi che questi strazi sono dolcezze per me, perchè ne faccio dono al mio Signore . . . Perchè, tacendo, io gli dò il tuo amore . . . Te, gli dò, Principessa, e perdo tutto!

even impossible hope!
persino l'impossibile speranza!

(*and, addressing the guards*)

Bind me! Torture me!
Give me
torments and pains . . . !
Ah! as the supreme offering of my love!

Legatemi! Straziatemi!
Tormenti e spasimi
date a me!
Ah! Come offerta suprema del mio amore!

TURANDOT

(*who, for a moment, has remained upset and fascinated by Liù's words, orders the ministers:*)

Tear the secret from her!

Strappatele il segreto!

PING

Call Pu-Tin-Pao!

Chiamate Pu-Tin-Pao!

THE UNKNOWN PRINCE
(*struggling angrily*)

No, accursed!

No, maledetto!

THE CROWD

The executioner!
The executioner!
The executioner!

Il boia!
Il boia!
Il boia!

PING

Let her be put to torture!

Sia messa alla tortura!

THE CROWD
(*savagely*)

To torture!
Yes! The executioner!
Let her speak!
To torture!

Alla tortura!
Si! il boia!
Parli!
Alla tortura!

And suddenly the gigantic Pu-Tin-Pao with his assistants appears in the background, motionless and frightening. Liù emits a desperate cry, wanders about like a madwoman, trying in vain to force her way out, imploring, pleading.

LIÙ

I can stand no more!
I'm afraid of myself!
Let me pass . . . !

Più non resisto!
Ho paura di me!
Lasciatemi passare . . . !

THE CROWD
(*blocking her way*)

Speak! Speak!

Parla! Parla!

LIÙ
(*desperately, running over to Turandot*)

Yes, Princess . . . ! Listen to me!
You who are girded with frost,
overcome by such flame,
you also will love him!
Before this dawn
I close, weary, my eyes,
that he may win again . . .
To not . . . see him any more!

Si, Principessa . . . ! Ascoltami!
Tu che di gel sei cinta,
da tanta fiamma vinta
l'amerai anche tu!
Prima di questa aurora
io chiudo stanca gli occhi,
perchè Egli vinca ancora . . .
Per non . . . vederlo più!

With a sudden movement she tears from a soldier's belt a very sharp dagger and plunges it into her bosom. She casts her lost eyes about, looks at the Prince with supreme sweetness, goes staggering over to him and falls at his feet, dead.

THE CROWD

Ah! Speak! Speak! The name! The name!

Ah! Parla! Parla! Il nome! Il nome!

THE UNKNOWN PRINCE

Ah! You are dead,
O my little Liù . . . !

Ah! Tu sei morta,
o mia piccola Liù . . . !

A great silence, filled with terror, falls. Turandot stares at Liù, lying on the ground; then with a gesture full of rage she seizes a lash from one of the executioner's assistants standing near her and strikes the soldier who allowed Liù to seize his dagger full in the face with it. The soldier covers his face and steps back amid the crowd. The Prince is freed. Then old Timur, as if crazed, stands up. He goes over, staggering, to the little dead girl. He kneels.

TIMUR

Liù . . . ! Liù . . . !	Liù . . . ! Liù . . . !
Rise . . . ! It is the bright hour	Sorgi . . . È l'ora chiara
of every awakening!	d'ogni risveglio!
It's dawn, O my Liù . . .	È l'alba, o mia Liù . . .
Open your eyes, dove!	Apri gli occhi, colomba!

In all there is a feeling of pity, of dismay, of remorse. On Turandot's face there passes an expression of torment. Ping notices it, and goes roughly toward the old man to send him away. But when he is near him his natural cruelty is overcome and the harshness of his tone softens.

PING

Get up, old man! She's dead!	Alzati, vecchio! È morta!

TIMUR
(*like a cry*)

Ah! Horrible crime! We'll all expiate it!	Ah! Delitto orrendo! L'espieremo tutti!
The offended spirit will avenge itself!	L'anima offesa si vendicherà!

Then superstitious terror grips the crowd; the terror that the dead girl, having become a maleficent spirit because the victim of injustice, may be changed — according to the popular belief — into a vampire. And, as two handmaidens cover Turandot's face with a white, silver-embroidered veil, the crowd says, supplicating:

THE CROWD

Grieving shade, don't hurt us!	Ombra dolente, non farci del male!
Disdainful shade, forgive! Forgive!	Ombra sdegnosa, perdona! perdona!

With religious piety the little body is raised up, amid the profound respect of the crowd. The old man approaches, tenderly clasps a hand of the dead girl and walks along beside her.

TIMUR

Liù! . . . Goodness! Liù! . . . Sweetness!	Liù! . . . bontà! Liù! . . . dolcezza!
Ah! Let us walk together one more time	Ah! camminiamo insieme un'altra volta
like this, with your hand in my hand . . .	così, con la tua mano nella mia mano . . .
I know well where you are going . . .	Dove vai ben so . . .
And I'll follow you	Ed io ti seguirò
to rest beside you	per posare a te vicino
in the night that has no morning!	nella notte che non ha mattino!

PING

Ah, for the first time	Ah! Per la prima volta
I don't sneer at seeing death!	al vedere la morte non sogghigno!

PONG

Here inside me the old mechanism, my heart,	Svegliato s'è qui dentro il vecchio ordigno
has awakened and is tormenting me!	il cuore, e mi tormenta!

PANG

That dead girl	Quella fanciulla spenta
weighs upon my heart like a block of stone!	pesa sopra il mio cuor come un macigno!

As all go off, the crowd resumes:

THE CROWD

Liù . . . goodness . . . forgive! Forgive!	Liù . . . bontà . . . perdona! perdona!
Liù . . . goodness! Liù, sweetness . . . sleep!	Liù . . . bontà! Liù . . . dolcezza . . . dormi!
Forget!	Oblia!
Liù!	Liù!
Poetry!	Poesia!

The voices are lost in the distance. All have now gone off. Alone, the one facing the other, remain the Prince and Turandot. The Princess, motionless as a statue beneath the ample veil, makes no gesture, not a movement.

THE UNKNOWN PRINCE

Princess of death!
Princess of frost!
From your tragic sky
descend down upon the earth . . . !

Ah! Lift that veil . . .
Look . . . look, cruel one,
at that purest of blood
that was shed for you!

Principessa di morte!
Principessa di gelo!
Dal tuo tragico cielo
scendi giù sulla terra . . . !

Ah! Solleva quel velo . . .
Guarda . . . guarda, crudele,
quel purissimo sangue
che fu sparso per te.

And he rushes towards her, tearing the veil from her.

TURANDOT
(*with rigid firmness*)

What are you daring, foreigner!
I am no human thing . . .
I am the daughter of Heaven,
free and pure . . . ! You
clasp my cold veil,
but my soul is on high!

Che mai osi, straniero!
Cosa umana non sono . . .
Son la figlia del Cielo
Libera e pura . . . ! Tu
stringi il mio freddo velo,
ma l'anima è lassù!

THE UNKNOWN PRINCE
(*who has remained for a moment as if fascinated, steps back. But he recovers himself. And with ardent boldness he exclaims:*)

Your soul is on high!
But your body is near.
With burning hands
I'll clasp the golden edges
of your spangled mantle!
My trembling mouth
I'll press upon you!

La tua anima è in alto!
Ma il tuo corpo è vicino.
Con le mani brucianti
stringerò i lembi d'oro
del tuo manto stellato!
La mia bocca fremente
premerò su di te!

And he rushes towards Turandot, holding out his arms.

TURANDOT
(*stepping back, distraught, frightened, desperately threatening*)

Do not profane me! — Non profanarmi!

THE UNKNOWN PRINCE
(*wildly*)

Ah! To feel you alive! — Ah! Sentirti viva!

TURANDOT

Back! — Indietro!

THE UNKNOWN PRINCE

To feel you alive! — Sentirti viva!

TURANDOT

Do not profane me!
No! No one will ever possess me!

Non profanarmi!
No! Mai nessun m'avrà!

THE UNKNOWN PRINCE

Mine!
I want you mine!

Mia!
Ti voglio mia!

TURANDOT

The torment of my ancestress
will not be renewed!

Dell'ava lo strazio
non si rinnoverà!

THE UNKNOWN PRINCE

I want you mine! — Ti voglio mia!

TURANDOT

Don't touch me, foreigner . . . ! | Non mi toccar, straniero . . . !

THE UNKNOWN PRINCE

Your iciness is falsehood! | Il tuo gelo è menzogna!

TURANDOT

Do not profane me! | Non profanarmi!

THE UNKNOWN PRINCE

My mouth I'll press upon you! | La mia bocca premerò su di te!

TURANDOT

Back! | Indietro!

THE UNKNOWN PRINCE

Your kiss gives me eternity! | Il bacio tuo mi da l'Eternità!

TURANDOT

Sacrilege! | Sacrilegio!

The Prince, in saying this, strong in the knowledge of his right and in his passion, pulls Turandot into his arms and kisses her frenziedly. Turandot — against such impetuousness — has no more resistance, no more voice, no more strength, no more will. The unbelievable contact has transfigured her. With a tone of almost childish pleading she murmurs:

TURANDOT

What has become of me? . . .
What a shudder . . . Lost! . . .
Let me go! . . . No! . . .

Che è mai di me?
Qual brivido . . . Perduta! . . .
Lasciami! . . . No! . . .

THE UNKNOWN PRINCE

My flower!
Oh! My morning flower!
My flower, I breathe you in!
Your breasts of lily,
ah! they tremble beneath my chest!
Already I feel you
fainting with sweetness, all white
in your silver mantle!

Mio fiore!
Oh! Mio fiore mattutino!
Mio fiore, ti respiro!
I seni tuoi di giglio,
ah! treman sul mio petto!
Già ti sento
mancare di dolcezza, tutta bianca
nel tuo manto d'argento!

TURANDOT
(*her eyes veiled with tears*)

How did you conquer? | Come vincesti?

THE UNKNOWN PRINCE
(*with ecstatic tenderness*)

Are you weeping? | Piangi?

TURANDOT
(*shuddering*)

It's dawn! It's dawn!
Turandot's sun is setting!

È l'alba! È l'alba!
Turandot tramonta!

DISTANT VOICES

Dawn! Light and life!
All is pure!
All is holy!
What sweetness
in your weeping!

L'alba! Luce e vita!
Tutto è puro!
Tutto è santo!
Che dolcezza
nel tuo pianto!

THE UNKNOWN PRINCE

It's dawn! It's dawn!
And love . . . is born with the sun!

È l'alba! È l'alba!
E amor . . . nasce col sole!

TURANDOT

Let no one see me . . .	Che nessun mi veda . . .
(and with resigned sweetness)	
My glory has ended!	La mia gloria è finita!

THE UNKNOWN PRINCE
(with impetuous abandon)

No! It's beginning!	No! Essa incomincia!

TURANDOT

Disgrace upon me!	Onta su me!

THE UNKNOWN PRINCE

Miracle! Your glory shines in the spell of the first kiss, of the first weeping.	Miracolo! La tua gloria risplende nell'incanto del primo bacio, del primo pianto.

TURANDOT
(exalted, overcome)

Of the first weeping . . . yes . . . foreigner, when you arrived, with anguish I felt the fatal shudder of this supreme illness! How many men have I seen turn pale, How many men have I seen die for me! And I scorned them but I feared you! You! Only you! There was in your eyes the light of heroes! There was in your eyes the proud certainty . . . And I hated you for that . . . And for that I loved you, tormented and torn between two equal terrors: to conquer you or to be conquered . . . And I am conquered . . . Conquered by a torment that I never knew . . . Conquered! Conquered! . . . Ah! Conquered more than by the supreme trial by this fire, terrible and sweet, by this fever that comes to me from you!	Del primo pianto . . . si . . . straniero, quando sei giunto, con angoscia ho sentito il brivido fatale di questo mal supremo! Quanti ho visto sbiancare, quanti ho visto morire per me! E li ho spregiati ma ho temuto te! Te! Solo te! C'era negli occhi tuoi la luce degli eroi! C'era negli occhi tuoi la superba certezza . . . E t'ho odiato per quella . . . E per quella t'ho amato, tormentata e divisa fra due terrori uguali: vincerti o esser vinta . . . E vinta son . . . Vinta da un tormento che non sapevo . . . Vinta! Vinta! . . . Ah! vinta più che dall'alta prova * [da questo fuoco terribile e soave,] da questa febbre che mi vien da te!

THE UNKNOWN PRINCE

You're mine! Mine!	Sei mia! mia!

TURANDOT

This, this you asked . . . now you know. Don't desire a greater victory . . . Proud of such glory, Go . . . leave, foreigner . . . with your mystery!	Questo, questo chiedevi . . . ora lo sai. Più grande vittoria non volere . . . * [Di tanta gloria altero, Va' . . .] parti, straniero . . . col tuo mister!

THE UNKNOWN PRINCE
(with feverish impetuousness)

My mystery! I no longer have any! You're mine!	Il mio mister? Non ne ho più! Sei mia!

* These lines were published in the 1926 libretto. Alfano originally composed music for them but they were cut, along with his music, for the first production.

You who tremble if I touch you! You who pale if I kiss you, can destroy me if you wish! I give you together my name and my life: I am Calaf, son of Timur!	Tu che tremi se ti sfioro! Tu che sbianchi se ti bacio, puoi perdermi se vuoi! Il mio nome e la vita insiem ti dono: Io son Calaf, figlio di Timur!

TURANDOT

(*at this unexpected and unforeseen revelation, as though at a stroke, her wild and proud spirit is fiercely restored to her*)

I know your name! . . . Your name! . . . I am mistress of your fate . . . I hold your life in my hand . . . You have given it to me . . . It is mine . . . It is mine! Mine more than my throne, more than my own life!	So il tuo nome! . . . Il tuo nome! . . . [Arbit * [Arbitra son del tuo destino . . . Tengo nella mia mano la tua vita . . . Tu me l'hai data . . . È mia . . . È mia! Mia più del mio trono . . . Più della mia stessa vita!

CALAF

(*dazed in intoxicated exultation*)

Take it, then! Death is also beautiful! Put me to death! Put me to death!	Prendila, dunque! È pur bella la morte! Fammi morir! Fammi morir!

TURANDOT

(*with growing, feverish excitement*)

It is dawn! It is dawn! My crown-girt brow must no longer bow before you! I know your name! Ah!	È l'alba! È l'alba! Non più dovrà piegarsi innanzi a te la mia fronte ricinta di corona! So il tuo nome! Ah!]

CALAF

My glory is your embrace!	La mia gloria è il tuo amplesso!

TURANDOT

Hear! The trumpets blare!	Odi! Squillan le trombe!

CALAF

My life is your kiss!	La mia vita è il tuo bacio!

TURANDOT

Lo! It is the hour! The hour of the trial!	Ecco! È l'ora! È l'ora della prova!

CALAF

I don't fear it!	Non la temo!

TURANDOT

(*drawing herself up to her full height, regally, dominating*)

Calaf, before the people with me!	Calaf, davanti al popolo con me!

CALAF

You have conquered!	Hai vinto tu!

(*He goes off upstage. The trumpets blare louder. The sky is now all suffused with light. Voices spread, closer and closer.*)

OFF-STAGE CHORUS OF WOMEN'S VOICES

In the light of morning, what perfume is released from the gardens of China! . . .	* [Nella luce mattutina quanto aroma si sprigiona dai giardini della Cina! . . .]

(*The scene fades away.*)

Scene Two. *The exterior of the imperial palace, all white pierced marble, which the rosy light of dawn has kindled like flowers. At the top of a long staircase, in the centre of the stage, is the Emperor, surrounded by the court, dignitaries, sages and soldiers. At the two sides of the square, in a vast semicircle, the enormous crowd acclaiming:*

THE CROWD

Ten thousand years to our Emperor! | Diecimila anni al nostro Imperatore!

The three ministers spread a golden mantle on the ground as Turandot climbs the stairs. Suddenly there is silence. And in that silence the Princess exclaims:

TURANDOT

August father . . . I know the name
of the foreigner!
(*and, staring at Calaf, who is at the foot of the stairs, she murmurs, finally conquered, as if in a very soft sigh:*)
His name is Love!

Padre augusto . . . conosco il nome
dello straniero!

Il suo nome è Amor!

Calaf impetuously climbs the stairs, and the two lovers are clasped in an embrace, wildly, as the crowd holds out its arms, throws flowers, joyously acclaims:

THE CROWD

Love! O Sun! Life! Eternity!
Light of the world is love!
Our infinite happiness
laughs and sings in the sun!
Glory to you! Glory to you!
Princess! Love!

Amor! O sole! Vita! Eternità!
Luce del mondo è amor!
Ride e canta nel sole
l'infinita nostra felicità!
Gloria a te! Gloria a te!
Principessa! Amor!

TURANDOT AND CALAF

Love! Eternity!
Love! Love!
Love!

* [Amore! Eternità!
Amore! Amore!
Amor!]

Final Curtain.

Selective discography *by Martin Hoyle*. For detailed analysis the enthusiast is referred to *Opera on Record*, ed. Alan Blyth (Hutchinson, 1979). The recordings here listed are in Italian.

Conductor	*Serafin*	*Erede*	*Molinari-Pradelli*	*Leinsdorf*
Orchestra/Opera House	**Scala**	**Sta Cecilia**	**Rome Opera**	**Rome Opera**
Turandot	Callas	Borkh	Nilsson	Nilsson
Calaf	Fernandi	Del Monaco	Cerelli	Björling
Liù	Schwarzkopf	Tebaldi	Scotto	Tebaldi
Timur	Zaccaria	Zaccaria	Giaiotti	Tozzi
Disc UK number	EMI RLS741	Decca GOS6224	HMV SLS921	RCA VLS 03970
Tape UK number	TC-RLS741	—	—	VKS 03970
Excerpts UK (disc)	—	—	ESD1003821	—
Excerpts UK (tape)	—	—	TC-ESD1003824	—
Disc US number	—	—	Angel S-3671	RCA AGL3-3970
Tape US number	—	—	S3671	AGK3-3970
Excerpts US (disc)	—	—	Angel S-36537	—
Excerpts US (tape)	—	—	S36537	—

Conductor	*Mehta*	*Lombard*	*Karajan*
Orchestra/ Opera House	**LPO, Alldis Choir**	**Strasbourg PO, Rhine Opera**	**Vienna PO, State Opera**
Turandot	Sutherland	Caballé	Ricciarelli
Calaf	Pavarotti	Carreras	Domingo
Liù	Caballé	Freni	Hendricks
Timur	Ghiaurov	Plishka	Raimondi
Disc UK number	Decca SET561-3	HMV SLS5135	DG 2741013
Tape UK number	K2A2	TC-SLS5135	3382013
Excerpts UK (disc)	SET573	–	410645-1
Excerpts UK (tape)	KCET573	–	410645-4
Disc US number	London 13108	Angel SX3857	2741013
Tape US number	5-13108	4X3X 3857	3382013
Excerpts US (disc)	London 26377	–	–
Excerpts US (tape)	5-26377	–	–

Bibliography

Mosco Carner has written *Puccini: A Critical Biography* (Duckworth, 1974) which combines rare psychological insight with musical scholarship. It is laid out in three parts (*The Man, The Artist, The Work*) to give a masterly and very readable survey of the subject. Edward Greenfield has written *Puccini: Keeper of the Seal* (London, 1958), and William Ashbrook has written *The Operas of Puccini* (Cassell, 1969).

The more general reader may be interested in the New Grove *Masters of Italian Opera* (Papermac, 1980) which includes Mosco Carner's essay on Puccini with entries on Rossini, Bellini, Donizetti and Verdi.

The Letters of Giacomo Puccini (edited by G. Adami) have been published in English (London, 1931).

The Memoirs of Count Carlo Gozzi were translated by J.A. Symonds (London, 1890). A general history of the *commedia dell'arte* is contained in *The Italian Comedy* by P.L. Ducharte (London, 1929).

There is no biography of Alfano in English. Many performers' reminiscences of *Turandot* may be found in Lanfranco Rasponi's *The Last Prima Donnas* (Gollancz, 1984).

Contributors

Mosco Carner is the author of *Puccini, A Critical Biography* and a biography of Berg.

John Black was Principal of Bedford College, University of London from 1971-1981 and is now Director and Secretary of the Wolfson Foundation. He has written extensively on the Italian romantic opera libretto.

Jürgen Maehder studied musicology, philosophy, theatre history, composition and staging in Munich and Bern; after some years of musicological research work in Italy he is currently teaching musicology and theatre history at the University of Bern, Switzerland.

William Weaver, translator of much contemporary Italian literature, has also published translations of other Puccini librettos, as well as several books about Verdi, and translations of *Seven Verdi Librettos* (Norton, 1975). He has recently completed a biography of Duse.

Acknowledgements

Grateful acknowledgement is due to Dottoressa Simonetta Puccini for allowing the reproduction of the photographs of the first performers and designs from the Istituto di Studi Pucciniani; also to Mr Alan Sievewright for advice, especially for suggesting the transcription of Dame Eva Turner's address, as well as for encouraging research into the original version of Alfano's ending (of which he and Miss Denny Dayviss promoted the first London performance). He is currently working on a film of the composer's life: *Puccini: In Search of the Immortal Bohemian*.